5 Steps to Solo Travel: Part B

A Woman's Guide to Destinations in Her Prime

by Dr. Mary Travelbest

Reviews about 5 Steps to Solo Travel

I was intrigued by Dr. Travelbest's honesty and sometimes hilarious lessons learned (you can't make this stuff up). Her clever approach to organizing topics based on STEPS of experience was very helpful to me reading through her book. -S. Holloway

This book was an inspiration to start traveling. Baby steps at first to build my confidence, but I'm ready to start exploring. The idea of starting close to home and maybe just an overnight trip before venturing out on a long journey is a great start. -Cathy Andreucci, Retired Dental Hygienist

Dr. Mary Travelbest's excellent writing got me excited about restarting my travel adventures. It's a great read filled with tools and tips that will help you become an expert traveler. -Shelly Palmer, CEO, The Palmer Group

For those of you who love the adventure of traveling alone and those of you who would love to do it but have not yet gotten up the guts to buy that ticket, I have good news for you. Finally, someone has written a great guide for traveling solo. Dr. Mary Travelbest published a fun book with great tips, suggestions, and other ways to make your solo vacation great. This is the kind of book that you will love reading and will probably buy an extra copy for your friends and family members that just love traveling. -G. Solomon, former FedEx manager

If you're a first-time adventurer or seasoned traveler, you'll certainly find tips and lessons learned from Dr. Mary Travelbest. Avoid unwanted travel hiccups in advance by reading this book before you go. You'll travel with a sense of confidence and comfort. -Cindy Clark

The combination of motivation and practical advice in this book will inspire readers to pack their bags and begin their next travel adventure! -Shareen Grogan

5 Steps to Solo Travel: Part B

A Woman's Guide to Destinations in Her Prime

Dr. Mary Travelbest

DEDICATION

Other books by Dr. Mary Travelbest

The World's First Guide to Independent Travel, 1993 (paperback, CD, cassette)

5 Steps to Solo Travel: A Woman's Guide to Travel in her Prime, Part A, 2022 (eBook, paperback, and audio)

Take this guide as one source of many. We make no warranty about the content's accuracy or completeness and disclaim all liability arising from its use. This is not medical advice. Seek professional help for this. For more information, please get in touch with mmccabe@sunmarketing.net

To be added to the mailing list, please send a request. Please review this book on Amazon and other websites, as the author will be very grateful. Join the social success on all platforms and invite your friends. Download the podcasts and bring Dr. Travelbest with you. With your help, together, we can improve peace worldwide.

Dedication

This book is dedicated to the women travelers who have blazed the path before this and those who will continue to do so in the days ahead.

CONTENTS

INTRODUCTION

To discover your step of solo travel, you need to identify the experience level you currently match and then consider the next step you want to reach. You learned about the steps in *"The 5 Steps to Solo Travel*: A Woman's Guide to Travel in Her Prime, Part A,"* which describes five distinct travel steps. To fully experience this book, choose your step, and select from the destinations you may have on your bucket list.

What kind of traveler are you? This depends on your health and financial circumstances. Part A of the guide will remind you how to find your step and learn more about this type of travel. You will identify yourself with at least one of the steps of experience, which may change depending on your current conditions. Be ready to move up or down to a new step. If you are new to travel, follow the steps in order. I've heard from thousands of travelers who did not plan well based on their experience level and suffered needlessly. Don't be like them: read the sections that guide your steps to your destinations.

Content design is for you, the reader. Highlight and circle the places you want to travel to as you read. Add sticky notes to remember these sections, and you will manage your favorite destinations. Some areas have more descriptions than others because I liked visiting these places more. This is written for you. It's the book you have dreamed about for years on how to navigate solo travel. You may settle in on a step or two and read those sections. Each state/country has five items, or STEPS, at the beginning. These are: sleeping, transportation, eating, packing, and suggested, where the first letter spells out the word 'STEPS.' Each section includes a personal Dr. Travelbest insight plus a Do/Don't. Look for future parts of this series. You can also listen to the Dr. Mary Travelbest Guide on your favorite podcast platform to pick up fresh solo travel ideas when you are on the go. Please leave a rating and review.

The 5 Steps to Solo Travel Recap from Part A

Step 1: No experience yet, but ready to start a solo trip. Your customized trips begin in a city where you have a family member or friend you can visit on your first solo trip. It could be Boston, New York, or even a rural town in Montana. It should be close to your home state for a day or two.

Step 2: Some solo travel, but mostly you know groups or organized tours. Suggested trips include state-to-state travel for an extended period, entirely on your own.

Step 3: You will travel solo to a distant state, such as Hawaii or Alaska, in the US or a nearby country. This list includes Canada, Mexico, and the British Virgin Islands. Suggested trips might include these places but with a more adventurous or spontaneous spirit.

Step 4: You've already taken several independent trips, but not in a foreign language environment. Whether you've been to Australia, New Zealand, Ireland, the UK, Germany (as most speak English there), or internally within Mexico, your next step is to experience a new local culture.

Step 5: You have been to many countries where they speak another local language. You have faced challenges like surmounting cultures yet to be familiar to you or navigating travel in a place where transportation is limited. These places are harder to reach, though not unwelcoming--here's to your next step! Examples: African countries such as Kenya or Asian countries such as Japan.

The following are more detailed descriptions of the STEPS.

STEP ONE

This is the place to begin if you have yet to travel recently. You may have traveled before, but it's been a while—or the entire COVID lockdown has limited your confidence about travel, and you need to jumpstart your engines.

Consider: when you were the new kid in school, you were starting a new chapter and knew it. If you realize you are embarking on a new journey, you will give yourself some extra time and grace to travel alone and learn. Ask questions along the way. Don't assume everything will go well (it won't!). Accept that plans will go smoothly sometimes; celebrate those moments. When you look back on your personal history, you will tell the story the way you saw it unfold from your perspective as a Step One traveler. Put away those memories from plans that didn't go exactly as you expected.

Step One is the first trip to a nearby place in the US. It could be a car trip to a city or town within a few hours' drive. On the other hand, you may set aside one day to drive to a new place and walk through a meadow when you get there. With each step you take without a guide, you grow in independence. Before your trip, research and use the internet, including social media platforms. While on your journey, talk to people. This is the crucial point—it's YOUR journey, not someone else's.

There's much to be said about having a companion on your trip. For many of us, having someone to share the fun with is a good idea. However, not everyone has someone to travel with. If you are in this situation, the best idea

3

is to start planning a customized, solo trip—just for you. Then, make your arrangements as if they were just for you, so you have no excuses not to go.

For more of a challenge, look at your destination's geography. Invest in a map, read your atlas, and use your smartphone to discover how to get there. Figure out the best time to travel, perhaps avoiding commuter traffic by traveling mid-day, and whether you will stay overnight. You don't always need to book your accommodations in advance, but you can, and for your first solo trip, that will help reduce stress and worry. For example, you may have trouble booking a hotel room in Yellowstone National Park during peak season. You may also want to stay with a friend or family for a night. You're in Step One! You can do this.

STEP TWO

In the next step, the adventurer may be eager to experience a healthy dose of new activities by taking a trip further away than one-night destinations. The destinations to consider might be in a nearby state in the US or wherever you live—but not too far away. Instead of staying with a friend or family member, consider a grander adventure by yourself. You are going to wander, explore, and experience new things. Be ready for a slightly different experience from the first step, despite significant fear of the unknown. Visit a nearby state, just a short flight or a 200-mile car trip away, where you might stay overnight for at least one or two days. After arriving at your destination, you might visit local sites using public transportation, such as the train, bus, or trolley. If there is a zoo, spend a few hours exploring it as a natural experience. Go to a park and walk the perimeter. Find a shopping center and explore new stores you have not been to. Try fresh food (or several!). Explore new tastes, smells, and colorful places to tease your curiosity.

To travel in Step Two, you will need to consider where you will sleep, eat, tour, and learn some context of the region's history. Take note of sightseeing suggestions from others, such as Trip Advisor. Visit your local AAA office, contact a travel professional, or book your flight through the airline. You can do this because you are already at Step Two.

STEP THREE

At this next step, traveling includes passport-required countries, international visas, and driving. Your travel has advanced to the middle point in the 5 Steps to Solo Travel. Step One was about getting started with a drive to another city. In Step Two, you went to another region or state. You are now at Step Three and are more accomplished than most travelers, even if you don't realize it. To advance to Step Three, you should have already visited different regions of the USA, and if in a foreign country, in regional areas within that country. You are now ready to explore more outside of your small bubble. You don't necessarily need a guide to show you the way. I recommend checking the Centers for Disease Control (CDC) and State Department websites before traveling to any foreign destinations at Step Three. The US Government's (Smart Traveler Enrollment Program (STEP) will be discussed in later chapters. Traveling outside the USA is a good idea because you can experience architectural and historic buildings, dine on local cuisines, enjoy local music and customs, and practice a new language.

Bigger Travel

As you step out into regions farther from home, it's time to focus on these regions' geography and climate as you plan your trip. The timing of your travel will be crucial to your comfort and enjoyment. The economy also plays a role, making supply and demand a determining factor—especially if you don't like being in a crowd. Step Three is for the more advanced traveler, so get ready for some more giant slices of adventurous fun. Here you will learn more about US states such as Hawaii and Alaska, where you don't need a US passport if you are a citizen. Canada is also in this category, and a passport is required. Airline, rail, and ship travel may require health passports, vaccinations, or proof of insurance.

At Step Three, you are becoming a more invested traveler, as you will not always be in a "known place" throughout your journey. For a US traveler, it means reaching far but not too many miles away. This step will likely include airline travel with weather similar to your current region, or you may find extreme temperatures. For example, the climate in Hawaii or the Bahamas may be mild and balmy or tropical. On the other hand, it rains/snows a lot in Alaska, so you'll need weather protection year-round. Other climate factors are hurricanes and different weather-related temperature and atmosphere changes. Review this before making your final plans if there is usually a seasonal temperature swing.

STEP FOUR

Step 4 is the second to last step of Solo Travel. It will be the final step for many readers, and getting here is a significant accomplishment. At this step, you are going long distances by plane, and generally, you can understand the local people. Traveling to a foreign country like Australia, New Zealand, or even Germany would break into Step 4. You may be wondering why Germany is on this list. You can travel to many European countries without speaking the local language. Most of the people there speak English as a second language. Step 4 is for the solo traveler who wants to explore new countries but is not proficient in the countries' languages. Like Germany, you may discover several European countries which don't require you to speak their local language to travel independently.

Setting a goal

You may set a goal for yourself to master Step Four. This is experienced travel. In this step, you are confident because you have already mastered the art of going places with your itinerary, even if it was just for part of the trip. You've learned through making your own travel mistakes and know how to recover from them. We've all learned from our lessons and mistakes. It may be challenging, but it's not something to complain about. During this training step, try not to repeat the same mistakes. Step 4 will still require courage and some planning, but you can plan a more spontaneous trip—perhaps, just a few days instead of weeks or months into the future. Step 4 might be a trip to Ireland. Here, you'll be driving on the left side of the road, which requires significant attention to be safe.

Most people speak English and have similar customs and heritage to other European countries and America. Gaelic is the traditional language, but most people speak English here. Finding your way around is increasingly fun and full of surprises in Step 4. As for currency, you can count your change and pay with local money by converting in your head or on your smartphone calculator. Step 4 includes these other aspects of visiting foreign countries. Understanding the language will allow you to quickly read maps, ride buses, and trains and purchase things you need, such as food and accommodation. Learning some of the local pleasantries in the local language, such as "hello," "please," and "thank you," can go a long way in building mutual respect.

STEP FIVE

Step 5 is an experienced and fully ready-for-anything travel champion. You are embracing unique experiences of geography and nature firsthand, even in countries you may not read about in the news or on social media. You will meet people who are different from you. Specific challenges will occur when you visit countries like China, where you can't read the street signs as other letters are used, or when you try to bargain at the fruit markets in Kenya. Step 5 is about going out and having unique experiences in nature, in countries you will learn about and see people different from you. It is the final freedom step of the five steps.

Part B Destinations:

5 Steps to Solo Travel: Part B, A Woman's Guide to Destinations in Her Prime, continues with more user-defined guidance to specific locations. In part B of this series, you can guide yourself to a destination based on your recent experience. For example, if you have never traveled solo overnight, this book suggests destinations you can reach by car, bus, or train at Step One, including cities like Boston, Massachusetts; Madison, Wisconsin; or Sedona, Arizona.

In each region/country, there is a quick summary of steps for each of the following: Sleeping, Transportation, Eating, Packing, and Suggested, the initials of a key Travelbest word, which spells out STEPS. The first two steps are organized by Eastern, Midwest, and Western destinations from north to south by states/cities. Step Three includes destinations outside the continental USA, including Hawaii, Alaska, and nearby countries. Steps Four and Five show countries with the same STEPS for each destination by country/city.

Remember that you are never really alone because God is with you.

1
EASY SOLO TRAVEL STEP 1

USA's East Coast, Midwest, and West Coast destinations are listed here according to region. Find an area near you and visit a nearby city or state. If you live in a country outside the USA, you can organize your STEPS and send them to me via Direct Message. They may be included in a future part of the book series.

Eastern USA

Vermont; New York, New York; Boston, Massachusetts; Hilton Head, South Carolina; Georgia, Florida

Vermont

Sleeping: hotel, Airbnb, bed & breakfasts
Transportation: auto or bus
Eating: Ben and Jerry's, cheddar cheese, maple syrup, produce, wine, beer, farmers' markets
Packing: fall weather includes layers: sweater, fleece and windbreaker, raingear and hiking boots, and binoculars

Suggested: Green Mountain National Forest trip, covered bridges, touring forests' fall colors, ski resorts

Vermont is for lovers, but what about solo travelers? It's ideal because it's a small and easily drivable state near enough to significant airports but without lots of traffic. There is scenery in every direction from your vehicle. It's ideal for the Step 1 traveler because navigating is simple.

Vermont is a small state nestled between New York and New Hampshire. To the north of Vermont is Canada; to the south is Massachusetts. In winter, the days are shorter, and you will likely cook indoors. Summer is accompanied by longer nights and fireflies, making visiting Vermont special. There are 251 cities and towns in 11 different regions. You can ski in winter, bike, and hike in spring, summer, and fall. Since COVID, Vermont has become more populated with New Yorkers, who have discovered more fresh air and lower population density.

Ben and Jerry's Ice Cream is my favorite stop for samples. The Factory Tour in Waterbury, Vermont, is accessible to people in wheelchairs, and listening devices are available. Tickets are sold on a first-come, first-served basis and only on the day of the tour.

Things to do in Vermont

Vermont has many food options, including farmers' markets and farm stands. Enjoy cheddar cheese, maple syrup, fresh produce, wineries, and breweries. Explore the more than one hundred 19th-century covered bridges in Vermont. People are thrifty in Vermont, and your money can go further here. Air travel is more expensive and less convenient, with smaller airports and fewer direct flights. Manchester, New Hampshire, has a recommended airport. There are no McDonald's or Burger Kings in Vermont—but the Green Mountain National

Forest in the southern part of the state has beautiful hiking options and plenty of locally-owned restaurants and coffee shops. The University of Vermont in Burlington is rated one of the best college towns in the country.

Here's a list of recommended places and ideas for Vermont travel: Killington, Manchester, Stratton Mountain Resort, Lake Champlain Valley, Stowe, Bed and Breakfasts, Vermont inns, and it's only a short distance to Boston or Montreal. The fall months (September-October), filled with fall colors, are the best and busiest times to visit. Consider the shoulder season (August and November) to avoid crowds.

Travelbest: I've been delighted with my Fall Foliage visits. I had to drive an extra 50 miles to find a hotel that I did not reserve in advance during the peak fall season holiday. This was a lesson learned.

Do check the weather forecast for clear skies and spend this time outdoors.

Don't expect to get the hotel of your dreams without a reservation during this season.

New York City

Sleeping: hotel, Airbnb, hostels
Transportation; rideshare, taxi, auto, subway, bus, train
Eating: thin crust pizza, sub sandwiches, Buffalo wings, bagels and lox, cheesecake, lobster rolls, Manhattan clam chowder, pastrami on rye, Eggs Benedict, Waldorf salad, Carvel ice cream, hot dogs, egg cream, ice cream soda
Packing: Fall or spring are best for travel with sweaters, coats, raingear,

walking shoes

Suggested: Times Square, Empire State Building, Statue of Liberty, Unisphere, Central Park, shopping, St. Patrick's Cathedral, Broadway musicals, baseball game, Staten Island Ferry, Ground Zero

What's different about travel in New York City? Is it safe? If you stay in open areas and pay attention to your surroundings, you should be safe in the city.

This is a Step 1 destination because this city has so many visitors. Locals are used to welcoming visitors as an essential part of the economy. The city's transportation system is well developed with various ways to move around, and walking to many destinations is encouraged. You can do many things in New York City because touristy things are easy to access. The city is accustomed to big crowds; for example, gathering in Times Square for New Year's celebrations is a local favorite, even in the bitter cold.

See a Broadway show

My favorite part of New York City life is going to Broadway shows, especially matinees. Try to go to different theaters on every visit and enjoy the musicals. Walking around the theater district is quite interesting for a traveler with a solo mindset. There are generally plenty of tickets to the theater for solo buyers, even for the best shows. There are plenty of museums in NYC, and they are easy to find on your own without a tour guide. The subway system is efficient and available, so travelers should be comfortable using it. The Statue of Liberty symbolizes the freedom each of us in the United States has been given. The Empire State Building offers beautiful views of Manhattan. It's less crowded in the evenings, and the city's lights are fantastic.

Central Park is a don't-miss part of New York City because it is 843 acres in size, located in the middle of Manhattan, and it's a free outdoor urban destination that defines the city. If you stroll through the park in the daytime, you will see many groups and families—and thousands of people walking or biking. In addition, there's a zoo, carousel, boathouse, tennis center, reservoir, waterfalls, ponds, and music stages.

If unfamiliar with the city, read on for a helpful history lesson. Here's an explanation of the five New York City boroughs: Manhattan is the lower part of the island. Shells worth about $24 were exchanged for real estate in the 1600s. The Bronx is the upper part of the island on which Manhattan lies, separated by the Harlem River. The Hudson River separates New York City from New Jersey. There's also Brooklyn, Queens, and Staten Island to complete the five boroughs. You may want to create a mini-solo trip in each section of New York City. There's so much to see in each borough as a solo traveler. Suppose you visit during baseball season, then head to a game between April and September. The iconic Unisphere from the 1964-65 World Fair, a spherical stainless-steel representation of the earth is in Flushing, Queens—140 feet high and 120 feet in diameter. If you're visiting Queens, don't miss this.

Travelbest: I was born in New York State, grew up there, and only traveled solo once I moved away. However, my family moved to Chicago in the middle of my 9th-grade school year, and my parents allowed me to buy a plane ticket and visit friends alone in the summer. It was my second-ever plane trip. I was nervous and frightened, but I knew I had to do this solo to see my friends. When I landed at the airport in New York City, I learned new skills, such as getting through the world's busiest airport solo, hailing a cab in New York City, and riding buses and the subway to my destinations. It was the beginning of life on the road. My favorite trips to New York City from Long Island were for baseball games with the Mets or the Yankees.

Do walk around Times Square.

Don't pay for any photos with the characters there.

Boston, Massachusetts

Sleeping: hotel, Airbnb

Transportation: subway, the subway called the T, car, bus, bike

Eating: New England clam chowder, Lobster Savannah, soft shell crabs, apple brown betty, Boston baked beans, fried clam roll,

Packing: raincoat, umbrella, boots, gloves, and hat in winter, lightweight clothes in summer, walking shoes.

Suggested: walking tours, cemeteries, Red Sox Baseball, Cape Cod, college visits, rowing regattas

What is so special about Boston, Massachusetts? For starters, it's a great walking city. The people are so real. Bostonians and New Englanders generally have an accent where the letter "r" is softer. Like Vermont, the best time to visit is in the fall to see the autumn colors. Springtime follows the cold winters. One in every five people in Boston is in college, so the city seems focused on higher education. Here are a few ideas for Boston activities: Red Sox Baseball game and tour of Fenway Park, Cambridge, rowing, historical perspectives, and fresh seafood.

Travelbest: The Boston Marathon 2013 was a disaster when a bomb killed people at the finish line, where I had planned to be on race day. This was tragic—a sad memory for the great people of Boston and worldwide. I had intended to be at the finish line. However, plans changed that morning. Instead, I was driving my rental car to Boston, listening to the radio describe the details with much sadness. Later that day, I flew home on a plane with the runners from my town. It was the quietest plane trip in my lifetime.

Do visit some historical sites.
Don't drive in the city if you can, as traffic is challenging on weekdays especially.

Hilton Head, South Carolina

Sleeping: hotel, resort, Airbnb
Transportation car, bike
Eating: Benne wafers, shrimp'n grits, Tiki bars
Packing: light clothes, bathing suits and flip flops in summer: jacket and pants in winter
Suggested: beaches, bodysurfing, biking, golfing

Across the border and a bridge from Savannah, Georgia, is a destination resort area called Hilton Head Island, tucked into a corner of South Carolina. The ocean water was clean and warm for swimming. You'll find North and South Forest beaches, which are family oriented. You'll also see dozens of golf courses, private beaches, and a Tiki Bar. Some public beaches in Hilton Head have beautiful water fountains lit at night in summer, and the parking lots are easily accessible.

Travelbest: Summertime I enjoyed the beaches. I was there on Labor Day weekend before a big storm was expected. It was muggy, and the storm was not as bad as predicted. Pay attention to weather forecasts, especially lightning storms.

Do bring your golf clubs.

Don't forget how close you are to Savannah, so stop there.

Georgia

Savannah

Sleeping: Airbnb, hotel

Transportation: car, bus

Eating: Cornbread, potato salad, peaches,

Packing: cotton and linen clothes in the humid summer, jacket for winter, umbrella, raincoat

Suggested: Tybee Island, St Patrick's Day Parade, ocean swimming

Visit St Patrick's Day, on March 17th, when the city celebrates its Irish heritage. The history of St. Patrick's Day in Ireland began in a cemetery in the 1700s. Visitors here can start with an early morning walk around the squares in the historic areas. You could visit the stunning Cathedral, Oglethorpe Square's art, the well-preserved architecture, trendy boutiques, and even hear ghost stories. There seem to be many cemeteries, hence the legends and ghost stories.

In the Savannah historic district, you can also find the history of the old south— like Drayton, Chippewa Square, enslaved people's quarters, and lots of original brick houses. You will see trolleys/tours, horse-drawn carriages, and a free tourist bus. Just past Savannah is Tybee Island, a destination to experience if you like the seashore. Tybee Island is a barrier island with wide, sandy beaches (including South Beach), a pier, and a pavilion. It's humid and sticky in the summer. Besides the beach, you can visit a few other touristy places here. Fort Screven has 19th-century concrete gun batteries in the island's north, and the Tybee Island Light Station and Museum have historical artifacts from 1736 through to the 1900s.

Travelbest: I went swimming in the clear ocean water, rode the waves, and delighted in the refreshment I experienced. On a hot day, you'll want to do the same. You may encounter trees with hanging moss in Savannah. I did. You should not touch this, because it can be dangerous. I was caught carrying some hanging moss, and a Savannah local asked me if I knew it was dangerous to carry in my hands. I had thought this would be a good souvenir. Well, I was wrong. Once the moss touches the ground, it may have chiggers (a type of flea) or even snakes in it. Birds use Spanish moss to build nests, frogs and spiders live in it, and boll weevils are drawn to it.

Do swim in the clear ocean water.
Don't touch hanging moss.

Atlanta

Sleeping: Airbnb, hotel, Minute Suites at the airport
Transportation: MARTA in Atlanta and suburbs, car, train
Eating: Cornbread, country ham with Coca-Cola red eye gravy, potato salad, peaches, The Varsity, Coca Cola
Packing: cotton and linen clothes in the humid summer, jacket for winter, umbrella, raincoat
Suggested: Five Points Downtown Atlanta, Olympic Park, CNN headquarters, Aquarium

Underground Atlanta comprises six city blocks of underground shopping, eating, and entertainment premises near the Five Points area. If you like to eat out, the restaurants have charming southern hospitality. You can get a Frosted Orange drink or a Coca-Cola at The Varsity, a well-known local fast-food chain. Stone Mountain is a hiking area to enjoy if you like to be outdoors—Trek to the summit in about an hour for this one-mile hike. Summers are hot. The Peachtree Road Race is a 10-kilometer run held annually in Atlanta, Georgia, on July 4th, Independence Day. The Peachtree Road Race is the world's largest 10-kilometer race. MARTA is the public transportation system in Atlanta, and it will help bring you closer to any destination you want. It's quick and inexpensive. Traffic can try your patience, and you can plan around rush hours on the freeways. Visit Coca-Cola on the CNN tour. The Georgia Aquarium is a public aquarium in Atlanta. It houses over 100,000 animals and represents several thousand species, all residing in 10 million US gallons of marine salt water. In downtown Atlanta, there are many universities. You can walk around the Olympics Park area from the 1996 Summer Games.

Travelbest: I've visited the state of Georgia since 1974. The neighborhood called Underground Atlanta is one of my first southern USA memories. It had music, restaurants, and a unique hidden vibe that was urban and exciting for me to experience as a traveler in a large city.

Do visit the Olympic Village areas in downtown Atlanta.
Don't get stuck in rush hour freeway traffic or expect to buy a Pepsi, as Atlanta is home to Coca-Cola.

Mistake- Passing my stop on the sky train to the airport gate.

I was on the sky train in the Atlanta airport, one of the busiest in the world. I forgot to get off when it came to my stop. Suddenly, I was back to reality; I missed my stop, and when I realized it, I got off at the next station. Then I had to go up the escalator, find the exit to the proper gate letter, and go back down the escalator. It didn't take long, but I was embarrassed that I had missed my stop. Don't nod off while on the airplane train to avoid missing your gate.

Alpharetta

Sleeping: Airbnb, hotel

Transportation: MARTA bus, car, train

Eating: Restaurants at Avalon, such as Ted Turner's Montana Grill restaurant,

Packing: cotton and linen clothes in the humid summer, jacket for winter, umbrella, raincoat

Suggested: Big Creek Greenway, Avalon shopping mall, Stone Mountain

Experience the Big Creek Greenway in Alpharetta, north of Atlanta downtown. The concrete trail is approximately eight miles and meanders along Big Creek parallel to North Point Parkway, from Windward Parkway at Marconi Drive on the north end to Mansell Road on the south. A soft mulch trail encircles a large wetland between Haynes Bridge Road and Mansell Road. Wildlife including blue herons, deer, ducks, and geese can be observed in this preserved water setting. It's suitable for biking, hiking, and running.

Travelbest: My parents lived in Alpharetta for more than 15 years. It's a place full of people who grew up elsewhere. In some ways, it feels distant from downtown Atlanta because of the variety of outdoor activities available.

Do bike or hike the Greenway.
Don't be surprised when it snows a few times a year.

Florida

Florida is a recommended destination for solo travelers because of the mild climate, whether you are a Canadian winter "snowbird" or want to have fun at the beach in Miami or visit the amusement parks in Orlando.

Sleeping: Airbnb, hotel, camping

Transportation: car, bus, train, plane

Eating: Key lime pie, white and pink grapefruits, oranges, fresh fruits

Packing: umbrella, raincoat, bathing suit, layers for changing weather

Suggested: Sarasota: Caspersen Beach Park, Siesta Key, Selby Gardens

Fort Myers: Ding Darling Wildlife Preserve, Mucky Duck Restaurant

Florida Keys: Islamorada, John Pennekamp Coral Reef State Park

Space Coast: Kennedy Space Center, Daytona Beach, Disney World's Epcot Center

Sarasota

Sarasota is called Florida's Paradise Coast on the Gulf. The closest you may ever get to Venice, Italy, may be Venice, Florida, an up-and-coming suburban area south of Sarasota. Travelers will find places like Oscar Scherer State Park, known for its beaches, bicycling, fishing, hiking, snorkeling, and wildlife viewing. A visitor center and a Legacy Trail are on a former railroad route. Lake Osprey trail is a suitable place to hike. It's wheelchair accessible and perfect for exploration. If you enjoy birdwatching, you'd love to spend some mornings here. Speaking of birds, the scrub pine forests are an excellent place for scrub jay viewing. A scrub jay is a blue-headed bird with a gray-brown back, a grayish underpart, and white eyebrows. It is said that the presence of a scrub jay gives viewers strong problem-solving abilities—who knew! Also, you can bring your RV or primitive camp if you like. The clear blue gulf water sand is soft and clean.

Beaches

Venice, Florida, has a public beach and a fishing pier beach. Caspersen Beach Park is more isolated. Take Exit 177 from 75 south to find Venice and beach bums with money. Downtown Venice is pedestrian-friendly, with free parking. The best beach for swimming and beach walking is Siesta Key, with water typically at 76 degrees in May and even warmer in summer. If you are an experienced swimmer, get into the ocean, considering the lifeguards' warnings about windy weather and ocean riptides. If you like orchids—or flowers in general—check out Selby Gardens. Each room or section of the gardens is better than the last. Meet and interact with people as you enjoy these colorful gardens. They're the perfect place to strike up a conversation for solo travelers.

Travelbest: I met Doug and Maxine Edder, who were 86- and 88 years young. They became my "friends" for the day, as I kept bumping into them as I walked the Selby Gardens. They were park-recognized donors, and I took a photo of them holding hands and standing in the garden named after Maxine. Naming the park was Doug's gift to Maxine on her 80th birthday. After that, I spent some time in TJ Carney's bar on Venice Avenue and got a pizza down the street with a friend named Jo Balsamo Wood, who spends her winters here. Hurricane Ian devastated the region with massive storms in 2022. Consider this possibility if you are traveling during Hurricane season.

Do visit the Selby Gardens.

Don't swim in dangerous riptides.

Fort Myers

Although struck by the 2022 hurricane, this region is an up-and-coming area for solo travelers and those considering moving to a warmer climate for snowbirds. Snowbirds like to escape the freezing and cold weather to warm and tropical lifestyles. This region is nicknamed the Paradise Coast for those seeking a better retirement from the northern US states. Be prepared for any weather here, as rainstorms can last 20 minutes or all day. The recommended Mucky Duck Restaurant opens daily at 11:30 a.m. Due to limited traffic lanes in each direction, getting there may take a while. Ding Darling Wildlife Preserve is a strangely worded name, but this place is worth visiting if you are in the area. It's a National Park, so use your lifetime National Park Pass available to those over 62. You'll see plenty of egrets and rare birds of all kinds here.

In Fort Myers, Estero Beach was a bit more commercial. Nearby Naples, Florida, is a town full of doctors. Driving through town, you will see many medical clinics and specialist doctors' offices. Medical services include concierge care, where you pay a fee for higher medical service. Many former New Yorkers have discovered this destination for their retirement home. The locals say people come here to die.

Travelbest: I drove into a rainy downpour crossing the island from Fort Myers. Fort Myers reminded me of Pacific Beach, California (mentioned in California beaches later), where there are vendors of all types of knick-knacks and beach bars.

Do a walk on the beach.
Don't forget to enjoy the relaxing moments here.

Florida Keys

Driving your car to the Florida Keys is a short journey from the Miami area and off the route of anywhere but Cuba, which is why many people never get there. Whether you arrive by boat from Naples, Florida, or drive from the southern Miami area, it's worth the excursion. Visit the John Pennekamp Coral Reef

State Park. Here, you can snorkel, scuba, kayak, or swim. There's plenty to do for those who like the outdoors, and you may find your favorite new activity here. The park also has glass bottom boats for viewing the fish if it's too cold to snorkel or scuba. This park is in Key Largo, the first key from mainland Florida by car. Here, you can easily rent a kayak and view the world from a new perspective for a few hours. Key West is the final island in the chain of keys, connected by long straight bridges. Many tourists visit here in search of excitement. Key West is known for spectacular sunsets and a thrilling party atmosphere, a la Jimmy Buffet. This is the southernmost part of the US mainland.

Travelbest: Of all the Florida Keys, I liked both Islamorada and Marathon the best because they were relaxing, with less tourism and smaller in size, and with a culture that was beach focused.

Do visit Islamorada.
Don't expect to find Jimmy Buffet on the beach.

Space Coast

This area has plenty of free viewing of outer space launches. In addition, you can enjoy 72 miles of Space coastline and beach fun for free. You may enjoy walking and swimming at Cocoa Beach in particular. Florida's Space Coast towns include Cocoa Beach, Melbourne & The Beaches, Port Canaveral, Titusville, Palm Bay, and Viera. Stretch out on the soft, white sand and rest to stimulate all your senses. Afterward, go swimming in the warm ocean waters. If you're a beach swimming lover like me, you can take an ocean swim here nearly any day of the year.

Travel in this area offers delights as simplistic as birdwatching and quiet relaxation. Of course, you can exercise by trail hiking and engaging in related beach activities. Here are some other suggested things to do: visit the Manatees, walk the 800-foot Cocoa Beach pier, hang out with the turtles, go shell shopping, enjoy nighttime beach movies on the sand, have lunch with an astronaut, or visit the Kennedy Space Center—the former home of National Aeronautics and Space Administration (NASA). This region relies on tourism, so you will find it friendly to visitors for the most part.

For military and aerospace history fans who prefer more structure in their travel experiences, there is the U.S. Space Walk of Fame and museums, the Valiant Air Command Warbird Air Museum, the American Police Hall of Fame Museum, the BCC Memorial Planetarium and Observatory, the Astronaut Hall of Fame, and Kennedy Space Center Visitor Complex. In addition, there is entertaining nightlife, jazz clubs, and a local theater in the region.

Titusville has the Space Coast Route A1A and is the home of the region's airport. Since the regional aerospace industry revolves around air travel, you may note that several airlines serve this lesser-known region, including Frontier, Spirit, and Alaska. For those driving, you will find Cape Canaveral in Cocoa Beach via Highway 528 West. For those who seek more travel adventures, you may try a new mode of travel into space. Even if you think space tourism may be years away for most people, you can still dream. Some readers will travel to other planets. You can sign up now to be on a space flight in the future - although that may come sooner to those with the right connections and finances. A bit further south, past the Space Coast, is Daytona Beach, a beach lovers' destination for decades. Cars are still allowed to drive on the beach sand, it is legal, and the sand is hard-packed. If you're a car enthusiast, you may enjoy this destination to view the many vehicles on the beach.

Travelbest: My first visit to the Kennedy Space Center was in 1974, five years after the first human moon landing. Hundreds of space flight launches have happened here since then. Space travel is our next frontier, so I'm watching the night stars more often and dreaming of space travel. I watched the TV show I Dream of Jeannie(1965-1970) based here. It brings back sweet childhood memories of a genie and the early days of the space program. I recently took a swim in the ocean at Melbourne Beach and wanted to nap on the beach, listening to the comforting surf.

Do visit the Cocoa Beach pier.

Don't drive your vehicle on the beach unless you know it's safe.

Midwest/Mountain USA

In this Midwest/Mountain USA section, destinations include Tennessee, Wisconsin, Nebraska, and Colorado.

Tennessee

Sleeping: hotel, Airbnb
Transportation: bus, train, car, scooter
Eating: barbeque, biscuits, corn fritters, moon pies, chicken fry, po' boy, Germantown
Packing: walking shoes, bug repellant, raingear
Suggested sights: Memphis' Beale Street, Graceland, Civil Rights Museum, Peabody Hotel (ducks), Pro Bass Shop for a view of the city, Mud Island, Highway 61 to Tunica for music
Nashville: Pedestrian Bridge, Downtown Library, Gaylord's Ole Opry,

Convention Center, Gulch District, Farmers' Market

Suggested activities: Memphis: biking on Mud Island, Nashville: walking downtown, especially the SOBRO (South of Broadway), professional and college sports teams, Broadway Street live music bars, country music

Memphis

When you think of great blues music, Memphis comes to mind. It's America's birthplace of great jazz, soul, spiritual, and rock music. Memphis' Mighty Mississippi river location has enabled the music to flow. Memphis-based FedEx Corporation must know about road trips because you can drive to many US cities and states within a few hours. This is a beautiful city to visit for Travelbest Step 1 travel. You can see the Civil Rights Museum, within walking distance of Beale Street, to learn about Martin Luther King, Jr., and his historical path for African Americans. The museum has a solid historical and emotional appeal, with videos, photos, and artifacts. It may awaken you to step into history - where Rosa Parks refused to move to the back of the bus and where Jim Crow's previous rules separated races. History comes alive in this museum through black art, music, literature, and publications. Visit the Lorraine Motel room, where Martin Luther King, Jr. was shot across the parking lot. This is the final stop at the museum. You may be emotionally moved by the experience, especially in the wake of the civil unrest in the US. There was so much to see in Memphis. You can walk downtown streets and discover why the city is a treasure. Nearby downtown Memphis is a neighborhood named Mud Island with a view of the Mississippi River bridges and plenty of visual experiences for a solo traveler. This area has a charming river vista across from Arkansas and is friendly to explore on a bicycle. The site has a paved walking/bike path stretching several miles.

In downtown Memphis, you can find live music on Beale Street at any reasonable time of the day/night. This is an activity to try for music lovers. Have lunch at the BB King Club and soak in the colorful, authentic atmosphere. On weekends, the city sets up 'no drive' zone barriers in neighborhoods near Beale Street so you can stroll through and enjoy its history and live music in downtown Memphis. Besides Beale Street, there is plenty to do in downtown Memphis. Walk to the city park dedicated to Martin Luther King. You can walk to the Peabody Hotel and visit the live ducks in the fountain.

For a more formal education on Memphis' music history, visit Stax Records, go on a Sun Recording Studios tour, or drive along Route 61 and find the historic Gateway to the Blues museum outside Tunica, Mississippi.

Elvis' Graceland tour can last up to several hours, depending on the tour and your time availability. Graceland is close to the airport, so it's easy to find and navigate. You can stay here in a nearby resort or reserve your tickets in advance and park about a half mile away if you don't mind walking and avoid the parking fee. You will hear Elvis' music. You'll see the house, the cars, and the glitz of Elvis' history of rock n roll. Even if you don't go inside on a Graceland tour, thousands of people have left notes on the brick wall outside the home where Elvis lived. It's a visual reminder with room for your signature alongside millions of others who have left personal messages to Elvis since his death in 1977.

Travelbest: I flew into Memphis on July 4th, 2020, just as dusk approached, and the fireworks all over the city were spectacular. It seemed like the town was a sparkling jewel, and I couldn't wait to get to know it. I stayed there for a week and returned a month after a 5,000-mile road trip for another chance to soak in the experience. This time I stayed on Mud Island. I saw many people walking -

some with dogs, riding bikes, and watching the sunset through the clouds. It was different from what I had seen on my previous visit to Memphis, an older, established neighborhood from the 1920s near the airport. I encourage you to get informed about the city's history.

Do listen to the music of Memphis with respect for the talent born here.

Don't get poison ivy.

Lesson Learned: Poison ivy and heat rash

Early in the morning, I had a telemedicine visit with a doctor who described my symptoms of a rash around my shoulders and neck. The doctor prescribed a steroid cream that afternoon, but the pharmacy never got the prescription. I called back the next day at 8 am and again at 1 pm to find no prescription waiting for me because they never got it, they said. I was feeling poorly. I went to the pharmacy and bought an over-the-counter cream to relieve the rash. I felt faint again and had to sit down so I would not faint in the pharmacy. Later, I called another doctor when I got to my hotel room. This time, the doctor correctly diagnosed the problem—poison ivy. I returned to the pharmacy, got two prescriptions, and began medicating. I felt much better after 48 hours. Although I still had bumps, the itchiness was reduced. The spots cleared up in a couple of weeks. They were all around my neck, chest, lower face, back, and arms. I got this poison ivy while hiking in Arkansas by inadvertently touching poison ivy brush It was unusually humid, so I was rubbing my skin with my hands and spreading the rash. If you have a rash, get help immediately.

Nashville

Nashville: Pedestrian Bridge, Downtown Library, Gaylord's Ole Opry, Convention Center, Gulch District, Farmers' Market

Suggested activities: Memphis: biking on Mud Island, Nashville: walking downtown, especially the SOBRO (South of Broadway), professional and college sports teams, Broadway Street live music bars, country music

If you like listening to live music, there's nothing like walking up and down the downtown Nashville Honky Tonk, with free entertainment, including live music. You may enjoy visiting several of these in one evening on Broadway Street. At sunset, walk the downtown Nashville Pedestrian Bridge, as a must-see in this city. It's just off Broadway and takes you to the Titans Football stadium. Nashville locals may point you out of the main path toward Printers Alley, with its decorative skulls, and to Bourbon Street, filled with New Orleans-style music venues. Find great restaurants around Germantown and the Nashville Farmers' Market. It's a local hangout with many distinct flavors, and you will taste some terrific wines from the region's Natchez Hills vineyards. The Grand Ole Opry is a few miles from town with the nearby scenic Gaylord Hotel. It's a conference center and hotel with stunning indoor horticulture and hanging human-sized guitars, making it authentic to the music industry. Indoor tropical plants, waterfalls, and plenty of windows bring light and color to the atmosphere.

Travelbest: My first trip to Nashville was a quick overnight stop on a high school bus trip to Florida in 1974. In March 2020, I decided to explore and see the region again. This was immediately after terrible storms and before the pandemic closed everything. Someday you'll be thinking about visiting Nashville, so here are a few of my thoughts about seeing Music City. I found it a great walking city, mainly because there was little public transportation. I think you'll like visiting it for two to three days. Downtown Nashville is easily walkable; I walked about 5 miles daily in the downtown area alone, even at night. I felt safe even after dark because the city is alive with other pedestrians. I highly recommend visiting and enjoying the street art, the food, and the music. You'll find something to do here, even if it's just people-watching and hearing live music on the way.

Do walk through the cities to see the culture and listen to live music.
Don't expect public transportation to be convenient.

Madison, Wisconsin

Sleeping: hotel, Airbnb, family cottage
Transportation: car, bus, boat
Eating: apple pie, Liederkranz cheese, beer, sausage, pretzels, apples
Packing: Fall weather is best, so bring sweaters. For summer weather shorts and t-shirts; for cold weather down parkas, hat, scarf, boots, and gloves
Suggested: Edgewater Hotel, Alpine Meadows, Summerfest, Madison Farmers' Market, Olbrich Botanical Gardens, University of Wisconsin, Madison, Taliesin East

Stay in the state capital, Madison, where the college campus dominates the city. The colors in fall complete the rainbow of earthly wonder. It's a couple hours' drive from northwest Chicago's O'Hare airport and half a world away from the hubbub of downtown Chicago. Consider visiting the 16-acre Olbrich Botanical Gardens, one of the top destinations in Madison. You'll find an indoor conservatory plus a variety of unique outdoor gardens featuring: sunken, perennial, rose, rock, herb, and wildflower. On weekend mornings, a Farmers' Market wraps around the State Capitol Building. You will find plenty of Wisconsin-made and grown products here. There's also a tropical conservatory. Frank Lloyd Wright's Taliesin East is worth a visit if you want a day to learn about architecture. He is famous for his designs and open-to-nature style of living spaces. Reservations are recommended. If you want a unique place to stay in Madison, look no further than the lakefront Edgewater Hotel.

After Madison, there is more to discover in Wisconsin. Besides being the cheese capital of the USA and known for its beer brewing, Wisconsin is a playground for solo travelers. It is an hour's drive from the Northwest suburbs of Chicago, Illinois. Check out the higher altitude areas of Wilmot Mountain or Alpine Meadows for the grand views at any time of the year. In spring and summer, consider visiting the relaxing beaches of Lake Geneva, Devil's Lake for camping and swimming, and Milwaukee for Summerfest, a traditional music fest near Lake Michigan.

Driving through Wisconsin, you'll see billboard signs for Wisconsin Dells. There are a lot of commercial activities there, including 90 restaurants, wineries, and breweries to visit—plus plenty of water parks. One of my favorite things is seeing the McDonald's restaurant in Green Bay, Wisconsin, which has many football artifacts on display with no entrance fee since it's a restaurant. Visit some area universities, including UW Madison, Lacrosse, Platteville, Marquette University in Milwaukee, and St. Norbert. They generally have reasonably priced sporting and music activities year-round.

Travelbest: I lived in the northwest suburbs of Chicago for ten years and frequently traveled to Madison, Wisconsin. My parents spent their 25th wedding anniversary at the classic Edgewater Hotel, and I love this city for a getaway.

Do visit during the fall season for the colors of the forests.
Don't forget that it's icy cold and windy in the winter, so bundle up.

Nebraska

Sleeping: Airbnb, hotels

Transportation: car, bike, bus

Eating: Omaha Steaks, Runza Hamburger, Valentino's Pizza

Packing: light clothes in summer, warm clothes in winter, including a hat, gloves, scarf, overcoat

Suggested: Omaha: Lauritzen Gardens, Lake Manawa, Fontenelle Forest, Durham Railroad Museum; Lincoln: University of Nebraska, Lincoln Highway, Pioneers Park

Omaha

Omaha is a city in Nebraska on the Missouri River close to the Iowa border, famous for its mail order Omaha Steaks, its pioneer history, and Mutual of Omaha's Wild Kingdom. It's a stop on the Lewis & Clark National Historic Trail, known for its history, museums, and cultural centers. The Henry Doorly Zoo and Aquarium spearhead conservation work and features a big cat complex and indoor jungle, rainforest, and desert habitats. Mutual of Omaha's Wild Kingdom, a documentary series about animal and nature conservation, sponsors the zoo. If you don't have enough time or money to explore the zoo, you can stop and ask to visit the gift shop at no fee; guest services will allow that. The Lauritzen Gardens and Keefer Park are perfect if you like rose gardens. You can spend several hours exploring these outdoor masterpieces. There are lots of parks, lakes, and rivers nearby. Other things to do in Omaha include visiting Lake Manawa, Heartland of America Riverfront Park and Fountain, Boyer Chute National Wildlife Refuge, and the Old Market neighborhood. Omaha's Fontenelle Forest is an easy outdoor woodsy hike, especially in the morning before it gets crowded. It's an excellent place for walking and hanging out, even during light rain. Omaha's Joslyn Art Museum is known for its collection of artists and explorers of the American West and is housed in a 1931 art deco building. You will find the Durham Museum in Union Station, a National Historic Landmark that will take you back to the 1940s storefronts near downtown Omaha.

Bridges to Iowa

Omaha is not far from Iowa, across the Missouri River. You can go "bobbing" on the Nebraska Bob Kerrey Bridge. This "bobbing" verb used in this part of the country is named after the 35th Governor of Nebraska and former senator, US Navy Seal, and Medal of Honor recipient. Bob Kerrey Bridge. You go "bobbing" when you stand in a designated location and straddle two states, Nebraska and Iowa.

Council Bluffs, Iowa, is quaint and peaceful. Cross over two bridges to get to the town. Manawa Lake is a treat to hike. Drive the South Shore Road, get out of your vehicle and walk around the lake. Here you will find the Durham Railroad Museum, which houses the famous railroad spike, as part of the Union Pacific Railroad, which serves 23 US states.

Travelbest: The Omaha Art Museum was closed during the COVID-19 pandemic when I visited, but there was a wedding party taking place outside, which I watched from afar. A mom and her teenage children were playing in the museum's fountain. My relatives from Ireland had intended to come to Omaha, but they never made it past New York. They stayed there because they found good jobs and a community that welcomed them. I've often wondered what would have been different had they traveled here in 1910.

Do walk across the Bob Kerrey Bridge and go bobbing with one foot in each state.

Don't expect to find billionaire Warren Buffet walking the streets of Omaha, even though his home is here.

Lincoln

Pioneers Park is expansive. You can drive around and enjoy the natural sights from your vehicle. You'll find a few things in the Nature Center in Pioneers Park. There are some excellent public golf courses where you can walk alongside. You'll discover Nebraska shades of red, especially red cars and many red barns. You'll see elk, bison, turtles, frogs, and 600 acres of prairie, wetlands, and woodlands. Nearby you will find the University of Nebraska, Strategic Air Command and Aerospace (SAC) Museum, Runza Hamburger, Valentino's Pizza, Lincoln Highway, and Rails to Trails Conservancy, connecting Lincoln's communities and preserving its natural and cultural treasures. This includes more than 157 miles of parks, trails, and greenways.

Travelbest: Lincoln, Nebraska, has always had a sweet spot in my heart. It's a great place to raise a family and enjoy the beauty of the countryside. I drove around the campus and downtown areas during my COVID-19 road trip and felt at peace in this fine city.

Do walk many trails.

Don't forget that Saturdays in the fall are football days for the home team.

Colorado

Sleeping: hotel, Airbnb, camping

Transportation: car, bus, bike

Eating: Enstrom's Almond Toffee (Grand Junction), Cane's Chicken, food trucks, breweries

Packing: outdoor sports equipment, rain gear, hiking boots, sneakers

Suggested: Denver: Red Rocks Amphitheater, professional sports teams, Denver Museum of Nature and Science; Fort Collins: Lory State Park, Colorado State University

Denver

Denver is a city of activities, so here are a few recommended activities for Step 1 and 2 solo travelers in Denver: Mini golfing or hiking, kayaking, white water rafting, skiing, visiting the Red Rocks Amphitheater, camping, biking, and watching sports teams—The Rockies (baseball) and the Denver Broncos (football). If you are in downtown Denver, you may want to visit the Market Street neighborhood and the 16th Street Mall area and the nearby Denver Art Museum, Capitol Hill, and the Metropolitan State University of Denver. In addition, the Downtown Aquarium and Denver Museum of Nature and Science are not far away, with a 97% positive visitor rating.

Fort Collins

Fort Collins, with a population of 165,000, is 63 miles north of Denver and a close drive to Wyoming. It's a vibrant city full of food, drinks, shopping, and Colorado State University (CSU). They have 300 days of sunshine per year here. You'll find houses built in the 1800s, a vintage trolley, specialty shops, and breweries. Some local museums have science, history, and nature exhibits. There is also a digital dome theater. If you travel west, you will find Horsetooth Mountain Open Space, known for its rock formations and Horsetooth Falls.

Downtown Fort Collins has plenty of things to visit, including the Exchange, the Old Town Square, New Belgium Brewery, Poudre River (pronounced POO-der), tattoo parlors, and restaurants. You can also enjoy kayaking, fishing, rushing streams, and the delightful Gustav Swanson Natural Area. Cherokee National, Roosevelt National Forest, and Lory State Park offer hiking opportunities.

Travelbest: My first trip to Colorado was in 1975, and I've been here dozens of times in all seasons, including a White Christmas meetup and family reunion, both of which included skiing. It's an excellent place to meet up with friends from all parts of the USA because of its easy-to-access airport location. I have several family members who live in the Denver region. I've skied at every major ski resort, many of them several times. In Fort Collins, I found horses one block from the CSU campus, hanging out at the barn while I took a quick walk in the neighborhood.

Do visit the Rocky Mountains and Red Rocks Amphitheater for stunning views. Don't get altitude sickness like I did when I tried to ski immediately after arriving by plane. Take time to acclimate.

Western USA

The Western States in Step 1 include Arizona, California and beaches, and Washington State.

Arizona

Sleeping: Airbnb, hotels
Transportation: car, bus, train
Eating: Indian fried bread, iced tea

Packing: layers of clothing, the weather varies from cold in winter to extreme heat in summer
Suggested: Grand Canyon, Flagstaff

Sedona

The permanent population here is less than 12,000 people. Visit in January, February, July, or August to take advantage of cheaper housing rates and fewer crowds. Hiking in Sedona is spectacular and easy to drive to, a little over 100 miles north of Phoenix. The incredible feeling of Sedona will rub off on you right away. It's a resort-type area, so be prepared for many tourists. The Grand Canyon is 90 minutes from Sedona or 30 miles past Williams, Arizona. This is the start of the south rim of Grand Canyon National Park.

Travelbest: In May 2021, I hiked here and could feel the heat. Ensure you have plenty of water, even for a short hike. Looking up at the sheer cliffs of the mountains makes me appreciate God's handiwork. I especially like the drive from Flagstaff south to Sedona.

Do visit some outdoor nature.
Don't get stuck in traffic on busy weekends.

California

Sleeping: hotels, Airbnb, camping
Transportation: car, bus, train, bike
Eating: apple pie, cioppino, Hangtown fry (omelet), salads, fruit, burgers, seafood, Mexican food
Packing: swimsuit, sports equipment, bicycle, hiking boots
Suggested: beaches, mountains, deserts, forests, Yosemite National Park,

Stearns Wharf

California Beaches (south to north)

From the south, near the California/Mexican border (especially Coronado Island), you can enjoy and discover coastal beaches until Los Angeles. California beaches are mostly "free" to visit, so check opening hours and parking before you travel. Watching the whales breach above the surface can be enjoyable, especially during the Jan-March season. Wherever you go, take the necessary precautions while swimming. Beware of shark sightings, and watch for stingrays at your feet if swimming in warm, shallow waters.

San Diego Regional Beaches

These San Diego County beaches are destinations for the Step One traveler. You can go kayaking in Chula Vista at J Street along the bay. It's easy to rent a kayak here for a few hours of effortless paddling. If you can, swim at **Coronado Beach** in front of Hotel Del Coronado. Ocean temperatures are colder than most east coast beaches in the summer. They can vary, but they rarely get more than 70F in the summertime, so expect some colder temperatures if you are used to warm Florida waters.

Sunset Cliffs Park has delightful waves and views and its rugged terrain. It's a great photo location, but not necessarily for swimming. **Ocean Beach** is a more urban hangout for the young and fun-loving. To the north, Dog Beach is where you can bring your canines and hang out with hundreds of other dogs in the surf. In **Mission Beach**, the wooden roller coaster landmark is often crowded in July and August, and it's worth stopping by for a walk or swim. Discover a beach spot where you prefer b traveling along the boardwalk to South Mission Beach. North Mission Beach and Pacific Beach are some of the best ocean swimming spots. Reserve a year ahead and spend a weekend at the Crystal Pier Cottages. They are at the foot of Garnet Street by the ocean. Hearing the surf waves crashing below you as you sleep is a once-in-a-lifetime adventure. **Bird Rock Beach** has great waves and is a windy place to swim, snorkel, and surf. For your safety, get expert advice from a local on how and where to swim in these waters.

La Jolla Cove is a swimming spot to watch the waves crash on the beach rocks during challenging surf. If you're not a good swimmer, inquire with a lifeguard before getting in the water. La Jolla Shores is an excellent place to learn how to surf, as the waves are often smaller. You may enjoy kayaking and scuba diving here, as well as snorkeling. **Torrey Pines State Beach** is along the coast with tidepools and whale watching January-March. Torrey Pines State Park is a favorite place for locals to hike. You can hike up the mountain and then down to the beach. Use the free parking on the residential street, or the State of California paid parking lots.

North Country San Diego Beaches

Del Mar Beach is an excellent place to visit if you have a leashed dog, except for June 16 - Labor Day. No dogs are allowed during the summer. The is a Dog Beach further north. If you arrive early in the day, you could park at 17th Street or 25th Street. There are good lifeguard stations along the beach for safety, offering a friendly neighborhood and paid parking. **Solana Beach** has a downtown area near the beach entrance with easy-to-find parking. Walk the neighborhoods to see Fletcher Cove, Sea Scape Park, and Del Mar Shores, all within walking distance from the train station. **Moonlight Beach**, located in Encinitas at B Street, is a favorite beach for locals and is open from dawn to dusk. It has volleyball courts, a kids' playground, and street parking. **South**

Ponto Beach, Carlsbad, California. South Ponto Beach is a wide beach in an undeveloped area. Take Coast Highway 101; the Batiquitos Lagoon is on the east side of the road. You can swim, surf, sunbathe, and play beach volleyball with your net. The sunsets are spectacular. It's located north of Leucadia, where the bluffs end. You will find paid and free parking if you arrive early in the day.

South Carlsbad State Beach and **Carlsbad State Beach,** also known as **Tamarack Surf Beach,** is from Tamarack Avenue to Frazee Beech, near Carlsbad Village Drive. Due to the North County San Diego upscale suburban location, Step 1 or 2 solo women travelers may enjoy swimming, surfing, scuba diving, kayaking, windsurfing, fishing, or just walking on the shore. You will spot people fishing and camping nearby, too. Purchase of a California State Park Explorer Pass either online or in person will allow you annual admission to South Carlsbad State Beach, Carlsbad State Beach, and several other beaches along the coast, plus parks throughout the state. Enjoy smooth flat walks on Carlsbad Seawall, a paved path that is four miles long. You will see joggers, rollerbladers, and bike cruisers here; the sunsets are memorable.

Oceanside

Beautiful Harbor Beach is Oceanside's largest beach, offering everything from surfing competitions to volleyball. The Oceanside Pier is worth a stroll, and looking towards the shore, you can spot the cute house where Charlie lived. It is now a pie shop from the original Top Gun movie. You will also encounter fishermen, whom you may join if you have a fishing permit. In addition, you get to experience swimming and bodysurfing in the ocean. Breakwater Way is a quiet, family beach located south of Oceanside Harbor. You can walk along the frontage path or bike for a great meal. Downtown parking may be at a premium, and you may need to walk 3-4 blocks for paid street parking. There is free parking at the Oceanside train transit station. The Oceanside Harbor, adjacent to Harbor Beach, has many amenities, including the Marina Inn Hotel and various shops.

Orange County Beaches

San Clemente has a train station (temporarily closed due to beach erosion) by the beach, close to the sand and the shopping areas. In addition, San Clemente has a daily routed street trolley; it's free for everyone during the summer (Memorial Day to Labor Day) and easy to reach the beach without worrying about parking and traffic congestion. Check out the pier for fresh seafood and clam chowder.

Dana Point has many beaches and is the world's dolphin and whale-watching capital. In Dana Point, sunset wine cruises, luxury spas, ocean-view golfing, and surfing are available. The terrain is flat, which makes biking easy. Study the map to observe how land juts into the ocean here. This makes it a good spot for whale watching. **Monarch Beach** is a residential neighborhood in Orange County with a private beach and spa owned by the Waldorf Astoria Company. The Monarch Beach Golf Course is publicly held, and solo travelers can make a reservation for 18 holes. **Laguna Beach** offers great views, the annual Sawdust Festival/Pageant of the Masters, and superb shopping. **Aliso Beach** is a famous sandy beach located in South Laguna Beach. One advantage Aliso Beach has is a large parking area next to the Coast Highway.

Crystal Cove is a California State Park you don't want to miss. However, it closes at dusk. You can walk the 3-mile length of the beach any time of year. **Corona Del Mar State Beach** is the crown of the sea. Locals call it CDM. It's a neighborhood in Newport Beach and a good swimming spot. It's at the foot of the San Joaquin Hills, on the east side of the jetty at the entrance to Newport Harbor. It is a half-mile-long sandy beach framed by rocky cliffs and a jetty. **Newport Beach** has two piers: Newport Pier and Balboa Beach Pier. The beach is 8 miles long and well known for its Boat Parade of Lights at Christmas time. You'll see numerous ships in the harbor—too many to count.

Huntington Beach is known as "surf city" and is named in several surfing songs like those from Jan and Dean and the Beach Boys. Its name originated from the founder of the area, Henry Huntington, a railroad entrepreneur. The waves are sound to surf, and the surroundings are beautiful. It's among the region's most expansive, cleanest, and safest beaches. **Bolsa Chica State Park** is a three-mile stretch of beach within Huntington Beach, including a campground. You can surf anytime and fish near the channel with a fishing license. **Seal Beach** is known for kitesurfing, beach surfing, and building sandcastles. It is in the northwestern part of Orange County. You can walk the pier, where lots of fishing takes place. You will see emblems of a seal all over the town. **Long Beach** is suitable for kayaking and seeing the Queen Mary Ship. I wouldn't recommend swimming here since there is no route for the contaminated water to wash out to the sea swiftly. However, you can go skating or bike riding. **White Point/Royal Palms Beach** has a bluff with metered parking, a play area, restrooms, picnic tables, and a view of Catalina Island. If you love fishing, surfing, or scuba diving, you'd love it here.

Los Angeles Beaches

Torrance Beach has 340 acres of soft sand at the foot of the cliffs, which extend to the Palos Verdes Peninsula. It has 300 parking spaces, restrooms, showers, bike paths, volleyball nets, beach wheelchairs, and swimming, scuba, fishing, and surfing options. **Hermosa Beach** is better for standup paddle boards because the swell is generally smaller - unless you're a standup paddler who likes to ride the waves. **Manhattan Beach** is a relatively reserved South Bay community. It's a wide beach and not usually very crowded. The pier has an aquarium, and you can watch the surfers from there, sometimes attracting a crowd. The sand is soft, and you can walk to restaurants and shops. Surfing and standup paddle boarding are popular here. With west and northwest swells, the surf is best in the fall and winter. Manhattan Beach is best for surfing and ocean swimming.

Redondo Beach is a coastal city in Los Angeles County with beautiful views. People may overlook this spot because Manhattan Beach and Hermosa Beach are more well-known. Paddleboarding in the Redondo Beach harbor is also popular. There is a fair amount of bodyboarders, especially by the pier. **Isadore B. Dockweiler State Beach** is north of Manhattan Beach and close to Los Angeles Airport (LAX), the largest airport in the region; You will hear frequent plane landings and takeoffs. Nevertheless, you'll also find parking, showers, and plenty of beach activities such as picnics, swimming, and biking. It's managed by the county of Los Angeles, even though it's a state beach in California. **Marina Del Rey** is a Los Angeles seaside community called "Mother's Beach." Lifeguards will monitor your swimming five days a week in the summer. You will find Santa Monica Bay and the Venice Beach area to the west. You can kayak here. It's a surf-free, sheltered beach.

Parking is costly, and bathrooms may need to be cleaned. It includes the boardwalk and public pier, which are usually hectic and congested. Venice Beach is in its bubble. You can find your bodybuilder here, and people watch to no end. There are many artists, palm readers, street performers, and a boardwalk for skating. You can find paid parking lots on Venice Blvd. This area is known for the following: pier, lifeguards, paddle tennis, Muscle beach, basketball, handball, Windward Plaza, and skate dance. **Will Rogers State Beach** is suitable for sunbathing, swimming, and snorkeling. Its beach frontage stretches for three miles. There's a bike path and walkway. There is limited access for the disabled, but you can find more information about this online. **Sunset Point Beach** is the northernmost beach in Will Rogers State Beach. It is situated in the Pacific Palisades district of Los Angeles. There is a hefty hourly parking fee, a guard at the gate, volleyball nets, and private homes. The geography changes here, and the ocean faces south instead of west.

Malibu Beaches

Topanga County Beach is the southernmost main beach in Malibu. You can swim, fish, and scuba dive. **Las Tunas County Beach** is quieter, and you can fish or scuba dive easily. Enjoy the serenity since there are fewer people around.

Malibu Surfrider, an LA County beach, has a lagoon and a pier. It features a mile-long stretch of beaches, 22 acres of wetlands, and dock fishing. Swimming is limited here. Park in the lot, on the street, or take the bus.

Robert H. Meyer Memorial State Beach includes three beaches, the best being **El Matador State Beach**. Get there at 8 am, and you will love it. There's a small parking lot and street parking on Pacific Coast Highway, also called PCH or Highway 1. Bring a blanket for picnics. Please slow down while driving there, or you will miss it. There are approximately 50 stairs leading to the beach, so you must be fit for this journey to the ocean. There are limited parking spots (50) and a nearby residential area. The other two beaches are **La Piedra** (walk north from El Matador) and **El Pescador** (north of there), open from 8 a.m. to sunset. While you can wander, sunbathe, and enjoy sunset views, avoid swimming too close to the rocks.

Lechuza Beach is a low-key spot in Malibu with a photo spot you will love. Parking is available on Broad Beach Road, but keep all driveways open. **Point Dume** juts out into the Pacific Ocean, forming the end of Santa Monica Bay. It has rocky coves, cliffs, headlands, and a vast beach. Solo travelers can easily hike the mountain path and see markers for the Chumash Indians and 19th and 20th-century sailing ships. Point Dume has excellent views and wildflowers and is a famous photo spot.

If you were to visit only one beach in Malibu, it should be **Zuma Beach**. Zuma is past Point Dume to the West. It has rip currents, cooler water temperatures, and white sand beaches during certain seasons. Zuma Beach has 2000 pay-to-park spaces, lifeguards, and volleyball nets. Dog lovers will be thrilled as they can bring their fuzzy friends along. If you love whale watching, you can watch gray whales make their winter migration from here. **Nicholas Canyon Beach** is a smaller and less crowded beach area in Malibu. It's a long beach and a great place to spend the day, with plenty of fun activities from surfing to swimming, fishing, diving, and even windsurfing. You can bring your dog but must keep it on a leash. There are a lot of picnic tables, 151 parking spaces, and plenty of room for sunbathing. **Leo Carrillo State Beach** is a northern Malibu beach with a large campground. There are several hiking trails to explore on the hillside.

Dan Blocker County Beach is named after the Bonanza TV star "Hoss." It is a tribute to his service to the community. It's a long, narrow beach between the Latigo Shores neighborhood and homes along Malibu Road. Paid parking spots and picnic tables are available here. Surfers, divers, and scuba enthusiasts love it.

Travelbest: I have visited each beach, so Step 1 or 2 solo travelers like you can enjoy your beach days in California. These beaches are accessible to the public, and the weather is generally excellent. I chose to reside in California because of its beaches, and I hope you enjoyed the descriptions. Tell me about your visits and experiences.

Do check out several beaches.

Don't get a parking ticket.

Other cities/regions of California

Santa Barbara

Santa Barbara is a city on the central California coast, known for its broad, sandy beaches, perfect waves, beautiful coastal view drive, and impeccable sunset views. It has a laid-back vibe, with a lot to do—and, fortunately, plenty of dining options to keep you pumped for the thrill. Hilton Garden Inn, Goleta, Los Olivos, and Breakwater Breakfast Cafe are my favorite places to visit. The pier downtown is called Stearns Wharf. There's a fun water taxi, the Harbor Ferry. Although Santa Barbara has had many fires and floods in recent years, it is still one of the most beautiful regions on the west coast. Look for the Funk Zone, named for the area that was warehouses and now features arts, dining, wine and spirits, retail, hotels, and unique culture. The University of California, Santa Barbara (UCSB) is located north of the city and has a beautiful oceanfront campus to visit.

Travelbest: The Mission of Santa Barbara is one of my favorite historical sites. My favorite restaurant, the San Ysidro Ranch, is way up in the hills. This is where I had a great meal on my honeymoon many years ago. We were told John and Jackie Kennedy frequented here in the 60s. If you're arriving from Southern California, consider rail options to come relaxed and already primed for the laid-back region with spectacular views from the train window.

Do walk along the harbor and the pier.

Don't miss the newer downtown area called Funk Zone.

Palm Springs

Palm Springs is all about relaxation. Ensure you have good sun protection, including adequate clothing and a sun umbrella. The area is known for its heat, spas, mineral water, and casinos. Wheelchair accessibility is top of mind in this region, with many elderly residents and tourists. When you drive along Highway 10 from either direction, you will see the windmill farms producing energy for the area. You can make a self-guided, ten-stop journey with information about the thousands of windmills between the San Jacinto and San Gorgonio mountains. Technically, they're turbines, not windmills. The Palm Springs Aerial Tram gets you to the high point in the area in minutes. If you like hiking, you will enjoy the outdoors and may even see snow in the winter.

Don't miss the Air Force Museum. There are two rooms, one from Europe and the other from the US. You could spend a couple of hours here. Wheelchairs are welcome. The Palm Springs Art Museum gives you great value even from the outside. The grounds have exhibits worth seeing. Inside, you'll find works from Chihuly, Picasso, and others.

Golf is big here in the Coachella Valley. The best-known course is the Indian Wells Golf Resort. Visit the resorts for the views, even if you don't play golf. If you play golf, you can find challenging and accessible courses, such as Escena Golf Club, Marriott's Shadow Ridge, or even a short visit to Seacrest Country Club, where you can play nine holes for an affordable rate plus $10 for the cart. That is an excellent price for the region if you count your pennies.

Coachella Valley is known for its date shakes for travelers. Stores like Shields, Hadley's, or others can provide that refreshment. An hour away from Palm Springs is Joshua Tree National Park. Unfortunately, there is little cell service in Joshua Tree National Park. The best view is from Keys View, where you can barely see the Salton Sea. The closest town is 29 Palms, a small, spread-out region with the Oasis Visitor Center.

Travelbest: Joshua Tree is in a remote area. The first time I visited, the temperature was 115 degrees F. It was so hot that I turned around and left. I've enjoyed some lovely spa days here and hope you can.

Do visit a golf resort for a view of the region and landscape.
Don't miss the Palm Springs Aerial Tram.

Lessons Learned- No cell service in Palm Springs

One of my errors was staying at a place with little to no cell service. It worked well that week when I hoped to get some needed white space. But if you expect to be in contact with your loved ones, be sure that the property where you stay has a strong cell signal. Due to the mountains and other factors, your carrier may need better service here.

Temecula

In the heart of the Southern California Wine Country lies Temecula. You will see lots of wine drinkers here, some in limos. This is a safe place to travel if you are on an all-day wine-tasting trip. The most famous wineries are Ponte, Leoness, Thornton, and Calloway. Old Town Temecula has many good restaurants, historical markers, and shopping areas. Solo travelers will enjoy walking the downtown Temecula areas to taste small-town hospitality in an up-and-coming neighborhood.

Travelbest: I've stayed at Pala, Pechanga, and Pala Mesa Resorts near Temecula. They all have a certain charm, so consider what you're looking for. The first two mentioned are casinos. They have very nice pools and some entertainment. Pala Mesa has recently been refurbished and is cozier. The restaurants here are excellent. I like the golf and the quiet peace here. A favorite visit to Oak Mountain, Temecula, was in 2021, and the view from the outdoor restaurant is the best in town. On a recent trip, I met the customer service specialist at the downtown tourist office. Their slogan is "Live Glass Full."

Do have a glass of wine here
Don't forget to tip your server.

Washington State

Sleeping: hotels, Airbnb
Transportation: car, boat, train
Eating: geoduck clam, huckleberries, seafood, coffee, tea, cheese
Packing: raingear, umbrella, change of dry clothes, layers of clothing
Suggested: See the list below, seafood plants and fish hatcheries, Washington State Capitol

Seattle and the Olympic Peninsula

Seattle is in the northwest corner of the USA. You'll see magnificent mountains, rugged coastlines, rainforests, small towns, great food, and culture. You'll most likely visit Seattle first and see some of these sites downtown and nearby. Here are some touristy places to visit:

- ☐ The original Starbucks Coffee Shop.
- ☐ Pioneer Square (old and worn).
- ☐ Pike's Market—Fish (Jack's), Chowder/King Salmon.
- ☐ Pier 39.
- ☐ Miner's Landing.
- ☐ Safeco Field-Mariners.
- ☐ Mt. Rainer.

You're only a ferry ride across the Strait of Juan de Fuca from Canada. Don't forget your passport if you plan to go across the border and visit the lovely Victoria, British Columbia destination. The Olympic National Park is at the peninsula's center, with the Olympic National Forest at the lower elevations. There are several rivers, lakes, and Indian reservations. Highway 101 allows you to travel around the area and pass through various climates, from cold jungles to Coastal beaches and marine sanctuaries. Here are some highlights you may find most interesting on the Olympic Peninsula:

- ☐ 101 to Shelton, WA, near the Squaxin Reservation
- ☐ Super 8 Motels and plenty of hotel chains
- ☐ Coastal drive: mountains, rainforest
- ☐ Fireworks for sale
- ☐ Casinos, such as Lucky Dog
- ☐ Indian Reservation: Skokomish River
- ☐ Purdy Creek
- ☐ Blondies Restaurant: where the locals go for breakfast and lunch
- ☐ Oysters, pick/steam/eat directly from the water if you live there
- ☐ Salish Seafood Plant-Shucking 15' piles of shells

Along the 101 near Quilcene, you will discover a Fish Hatchery where 600,000 baby salmon get released into the river every May. Eighteen months later, the fish returned to the region. Although there are no tours available, you may find this of interest. Washington's state capital is in the southeast corner of the peninsula and is accessible without a tour guide, where you can visit, walk, and explore on your own. It's located directly on the magnificent Puget Sound and is free to tour.

Travelbest: I've visited these places mentioned and recommend some outdoor activities you can enjoy, especially seeing the State Capitol and the House of Congress. Many of my visits have been in the summer months. I plan to spend more time here in the future.

Do eat seafood.

Don't forget your passport if you plan to visit Victoria, Canada.

2
MODERATE SOLO TRAVEL STEP 2

This chapter includes my favorite USA National Parks, Midwest and Southern USA, Western USA, Disneyland, and California Adventure.

USA National Parks

Sleeping: tent or RV camping, hotel, motel, Airbnb

Transportation: car, bus, shuttle, bike, van

Eating: restaurants, cafeterias, stores, picnics, diners

Packing: warm clothes, waterproof items, hiking shoes, layered clothing

Suggested: annual pass, senior lifetime pass (62 years+)

Why should you visit national parks? National parks are the United States national heritage. Whether a local or foreign visitor, you will love America more after spending quality time in a national park. In addition, the national parks have value for independent and solo travelers who like nature and outdoor activities. If you are over 62, you can get a lifetime pass, so go ahead and get it once you qualify. Here are the current requirements to get a lifetime pass:

- ☐ $80 per senior lifetime pass, plus a $10 handling fee.
- ☐ It applies to U.S. citizens or permanent residents aged 62 or over.
- ☐ You can obtain your lifetime pass in person at a federal recreation site or through the mail using the application form.

This chapter will discuss several USA National Parks, including Yosemite, Yellowstone, Grand Canyon, Bryce Canyon, and Zion. Please note that you may also find lodging outside the park if it is unavailable inside. The summer months are the busiest for travel in these parks.

Yosemite National Park, California

Yosemite National Park is in California's Sierra Nevada Mountains. It's famous for its giant, ancient sequoia trees, Tunnel View, the iconic vista of towering Bridalveil Fall, and the granite cliffs of El Capitan and Half Dome. In Yosemite Village, you'll discover shops, restaurants, lodging, the Yosemite Museum, and the Ansel Adams Gallery, with prints of the photographer's renowned black-and-white landscapes of the area. You can ride the buses around the park all day long. The Ahwahnee Hotel has a big fireplace that you will enjoy indoors. Guided horseback riding is worthwhile in Yosemite if you plan it on a day when the weather is suitable. The food in the Yosemite cafeteria is fresh and tasty, especially the pancakes. Be careful with the local scavenging squirrels; they are not afraid of humans. Yosemite hiking around the flat areas is less strenuous than the steep climbs, and the flat areas are suitable for wheelchairs. Here are some quoted reviews about Yosemite:

- "A perfect place to get away from work or anything causing stress."

- "Long hikes, wear comfortable shoes, and bring enough water and food."

- "Regular sedentary people will find it as enjoyable as the hiking athletes."

Travelbest: I rode the free Yosemite buses inside the park all day on a stormy and rainy day. I could see a lot from the window. I also went into the hotel and sat by the fireplace; the Ahwahnee Hotel is a delightful place to relax and read a book if you must be indoors. The Ansel Adams Gallery carried my first travel book, and I conducted a book signing there while pregnant with child #1. I have memories of camping in tents, sleeping in the car when the campsites were flooded out, getting engaged to be married in the middle of a snowstorm after hiking for 8 hours, and not being able to climb higher because of snow too deep. The squirrels ate through my sturdy backpack for a PB&J sandwich. Seeing how the squirrel ate through several inches of my heavy-duty REI backpack while I was sitting a few feet away was a shock. I traveled here with all four children and my husband each spring.

Do visit the best waterfalls when hiking, especially in May.
Don't let the summer crowds get you down.

Grand Canyon, Arizona

The Grand Canyon is best accessed from the south, in Arizona. It's a more extended trip than it seems on the map, so give yourself plenty of time to enjoy the area after you arrive. You will want to watch the sunrise, so dress appropriately in layers to experience the break of the day.

Travelbest: I've been here six times since 1982 when I moved cross-country. I stayed in a motel, Bright Angel Lodge, which is still there, although it has been renovated.

Yellowstone Park, Wyoming

Over 2 million acres of land make up Yellowstone National Park. If you like nature, this is the place to be. You will encounter as much wildlife as you want. The best animals wake up before us humans, and you must get up early to see them. The Old Faithful geyser goes off every hour and a half, and you don't want to miss the spectacle; the times are listed in the Information Center and stores. The entrance on the park's west side is closest to the geyser. Be sure to have enough gas and tank up when you can. Once inside Yellowstone Park, hiking Mt. Washburn, in the northwest section, is worth it. One of the downsides of this park is the absence of cell service from AT&T, and while Verizon was better, no carrier had perfect service at the time of this writing. You may need to work at getting good service as it is a Wi-Fi-challenged area.

Travelbest: I almost ran out of gas twice inside this vast park. Inside Yellowstone Park, northwest section, hiking Mt. Washburn was a highlight. I walked from 8859 ft. elevation (the Duravan Pass) to 10,243 ft, with several parts covered in snow, mud, and 70 mph winds at the peak. It took about two hours. Many of my best adventures were unplanned. I encountered much rain each time I visited and found entertainment in several dry locations within the park while the rain beat down on my tent.

Bryce Canyon, Utah

This is one of the most popular National Parks due to the scenery of the Utah terrain, including unique broken-arch rock spire formations known as hoodoos. The park spans 56 square miles in southern Utah. Try Ruby's Diner in Bryce, Utah, for the Cowboy Buffet and the 18-mile Scenic drive one way in the park. The drive starts at the Bryce amphitheater along UT-63. It takes you to the narrow wedge of the Paunsaugunt Plateau. The altitude ranges from 7,000'-9,100 ft during this drive. All the main pullouts are along the eastern side of the road. You can drive down to Rainbow Point and then meander back to the Amphitheater, stopping to enjoy the view whenever possible. Going south to north will simplify your entry into each parking pullout. You may see several tour buses while driving down this road on your solo trip.

Travelbest: I made several stops to admire nature, then hiked the following day at 6 a.m. I met several European college students hanging out; they shared some great travel stories and adventures.

Do go to Ruby's Diner for the Cowboy Buffet.
Don't forget you are at a high altitude, so pace your hiking accordingly.

Zion National Park, Utah

Zion National Park is worth visiting, whether you are coming from near or far. It's close enough to Southern California, where you can leave home at 3 a.m. and still get to hike on your travel day. A limited number of cars are allowed inside the park. From April through November, the free park shuttle is slow and the preferred option compared to driving. No cars go past Canyon Junction except to the lodge. The lodge is a nice resting spot if you watch the natural beauty from an easy chair. Once in the park, you can take off your shoes, do the Riverwalk, and wade through chilled water, which is delightful when it's hot. You will see Grand Canyon-like views here. Water falling over sheer precipices sounds nice, and it looks even better. Look for "The Narrows" This is a refreshing hike; you can go as far as you want and then turn back. Be sure to check weather conditions and wear layered clothing.

Travelbest: Temperatures in June at 7 am were 92 degrees. Observation Point was a 3-hour round-trip hike for me. Your time may be different.

Do hike early in the morning if possible.

Don't miss any of the stunning views.

Midwest and Southern USA

This section includes Iowa, Ohio, Texas, Arkansas, Mississippi, Missouri, Minnesota, Oklahoma, North and South Dakota, and Kansas.

Iowa City, Iowa

Sleeping: hotel, Airbnb
Transportation: car, bus
Eating: corn, beef, vegan food
Packing: layers, hiking boots
Suggested: Coralville Dam, Prairie Lights bookstore, Universities, Devonian Fossil Gorge, University of Iowa football stadium

Iowa City is full of what's best in Iowa. Corn, beef, and football are favorites. It's located in the eastern part of the state, about a 4-hour drive from Chicago. The Iowa Hawkeyes rule the region for Big 10 Football on Saturdays in the fall, with a university feeling which makes this a retreat for many Midwesterners. My sister has lived here for decades, so I visit her often. The concerts and music are second to none for entertainment. It's also a United Nations Educational,

Scientific, and Cultural (UNESCO) City of Literature. The people are genuine and hard-working in many ways. They suffer through a harsh winter and come outside feeling refreshed in the spring.

Devonian Fossil Gorge is a great place to explore the outdoors. This gorge was formed by two floods, in 1993 and 2005. Previously, it was a campground; now, it is a fossil bed where you can see remnants of sea animals from 375 million years ago. Cross the Coralville Dam and stop at the Visitor Center. It will help if you wear hiking boots or athletic shoes. You'll like seeing what has been buried in nature for so long, now visible thanks to massive floods in the area.

Take the Iowa Avenue Literary Walk downtown Iowa City and visit the famous Prairie Lights bookstore. Prairie Lights Books and Cafe is at 15 South Dubuque Street, Iowa City. It is one of the best bookstores; it has been around for 45 years, is nationally respected and internationally known, and has a tradition of serving the region.

After the bookstore visit, head outdoors. If you are an owl-lover, you'll enjoy them near Iowa City, where birds are protected and the public is invited. Bird watching and being outside in the fresh air are popular activities at the Terry Trueblood Recreation Area. The state's first Capitol, the Old Capitol Building, now houses a local history museum. The adjacent University of Iowa Museum of Natural History features prehistoric stone tools and taxidermy. By the Iowa River, City Park has ponds and sports facilities. The Herbert Hoover Presidential Library/Museum showcases objects and photos tracing the life of the 31st U.S. president.

Travelbest: I recommend a visit here to see unique geological wonders. I found a seashell embedded in a rock in the Devonian Fossil Gorge.

Do walk around the University of Iowa campus.

Don't miss some of the nature in Iowa.

Dayton, Ohio

Sleeping: hotel, Airbnb

Transportation: car, train, bus, plane

Eating: Milano's sub sandwiches, Oregon District, Pine Club

Packing: coats in winter, light clothing in hot summers

Suggested: US Air Force Museum, University of Dayton, Carillon Park

In the southwest corner of Ohio sits a rustbelt city with a population of 140,000. It's worth your visit to learn more about the Wright Brothers, the famous inventors who had their renowned bike shop in Dayton. Visit the Woodland Cemetery to see where Orville, Wilbur, and their sister are interred. Visit the Birthplace of Aviation. The National Museum of the US Airforce is a much more extensive experience than you may expect. It's easy to find, visit and even spend a whole day looking at aviation from the perspective of our military. Many famous planes are located here. Admission and parking are free.

In Dayton, find the Carillon Historical Park, with more than just bells. It's a 65-acre open history museum, open every day of the year, and has a lot to explore. Dozens of museum buildings and countless artifacts will inspire you. You will discover a lot to do for an afternoon, including many hands-on exhibits and a tasty restaurant, and learn about the floods of 1913 and how Dayton came to be after this disaster. Dayton's Oregon District can be a fun place to eat and drink in the community. It's a 12-block district that combines commercial and residential living, including many excellent pubs and restaurants.

Travelbest: The University of Dayton is my undergraduate alma mater. My favorite college basketball team is the Flyers. The school is known for its solid Christian faith in higher education and is one of the "happiest colleges" in the USA. Students excel in areas including Engineering, Education, and Communications. Riverwalk and Xenia are some of my favorite hiking areas in the region. My favorite Dayton restaurant is Milano's.

Do visit the history of the Wright Brothers' bike shop.
Don't forget to bring cash to the Pine Club restaurant. They don't take credit cards.

Texas

Sleeping: hotel, Airbnb
Transportation: car, train, bus, light rail, rideshare, taxi, bike
Eating: steakhouses, fajitas, fried shrimp, pho, crawfish, tofu, fried chicken, burgers, Barbeque, gyros, Tex-Mex, ribs
Packing: light jacket, light clothes in summer, warmer jacket in winter
Suggested: Galleria, NASA, Museum District, Rice University, wildflowers, farmers' markets, dance halls

Houston

Houston is a vast city, and the locals know it's been "underrated" for many years. It's a big city geographically, so getting around takes longer than you may imagine. For music, think Beyoncé. Literature is significant—think Larry McMurtry. You can shop at the Galleria, with 400+ stores, including 60 local ones. Oil is big in Houston, and the George Bush family lives here. The Johnson Space Center-NASA is a recommended tourist attraction. This is another home of space travel, like the one in Florida, only without the liftoffs.

Travelbest: I was stranded overnight at the Houston airport due to bad weather. I spent all weekend traveling, including circling Atlanta and landing in New Orleans for night number two. I never got to my destination, even though my bags did. I got my bags returned a few days later. I returned home without arriving at my planned destination, with a two-day visit to Houston as a reminder that plans are all subject to change.

Do see Johnson Space Center for NASA tours.
Don't expect to drive across town quickly due to traffic and congestion.

Austin

The city of Austin is different from other cities in Texas because, to the natives, most people who live in Austin are not really "Texans." Instead, most residents of Austin are from different regions of the USA, imported from places like California. The Texas State Capitol Visitor's Center should be your first destination, and it's in a downtown historical building with helpful information. The State Capitol is free to visit and has guided tours. Your next stop may be the University of Texas neighborhood; it draws you in, located off Guadalupe Street, with charming older and modern buildings with Texas charm.

In the springtime, Texas wildflowers are in bloom. If you are there to enjoy the blankets of colors on fields and roadways, you will be delighted with the abundance. From Texas Bluebonnets to Indian paintbrush and 5,000 species of flowering plants. Texas has a wide selection of flowers, especially in Austin. Visit Lady Bird Johnson Wildflower Center to see native plants in well-cared-for gardens and stroll around at your pleasure for an afternoon or all day.

Want to go for some live music and line dancing? Go to The Broken Spoke, the last of the Texas dance halls, established in 1964. Live music, dance lessons, and decent food and drinks are here. You may see bands such as 'Sentimental Family,' with musicians playing the fiddle, folk guitar, bass, and drums. The food on the menu includes fried chicken. Neon bar signs and music history all around the place, a one-story building with a lot of local charm and love.

Austin is famous for bats during certain seasons, from late March through early fall. The night flights begin after sunset when the bats fly out from under the bridges. There are 32 bat species in Texas. Bats avoid light because of predators; Be sure to avoid shining a flashlight or camera flash or touching them.

Hit up the Mueller's Farmer's Market on Sundays if you are in the central area of Austin. Hill Country is worth a visit, but like everything else in this area, it is enormous. Explore the Texas Hill Country for a few days if you like the prairies. Lockhart has barbeque, music, and breweries and is an escape from the city. It's an old cowboy town, part of the Chisholm trail, 30 minutes south of Austin.

New Braunfels is also located south, with antique shops, boutiques, and festivals. Check out the German-Texan town of New Braunfels and Gruene.

Gruene (pronounced Green) is part of New Braunfels, a small, relaxed, and quaint town. It's a cotton-producing community along the Guadalupe River. The Music Hall features a list of who's who; stop in and see some live music if you can. Yes, the town is full of tourists, but if you go off-season, as I did in January, there might not be anyone around. You can go window shopping downtown and get the town's flavor quickly.

Travelbest: I was fortunate enough to see some live country western music and enjoy dancing and singing at my favorite regional places. My favorite solo hangout in Austin is the downtown public library, with its 6th-floor rooftop where you can sit and read outdoors or indoors, depending on the weather. The tasty Black's Ribs are delicious; be sure you get the meat without the bone attached because that's where the price is sky high. Plenty of other places for ribs exist, but none are as authentic.

Do enjoy the Texas flowers.

Don't shine a flashlight on the bats under any bridges.

Little Rock, Arkansas

Sleeping: hotel, camping, motel

Transportation: car, bus, train

Eating: Barbeque, fried catfish, wild duck, rice, purple hull peas, okra, apples, grits

Packing: shorts and t-shirts in summer. Cooler in winter: jacket, long sleeve shirts, jeans

Suggested: Riverfront Park, Liberty Bell, Nine Civil Rights Memorial, Big Dam Bridge

Little Rock, Arkansas, has a lot of bridges, rivers, and lakes. If you walk in

Riverfront Park, you will see restored homes at the historic Arkansas Museum. You can ride the River Rail electric streetcar. The State Capitol has a replica of the Liberty Bell, the Little Rock Nine Civil Rights Memorial, and the Confederate War Prisoners Memorial. The Big Dam Bridge is the country's longest bicycle and pedestrian bridge, connecting 20 miles of Riverside trails. The Arkansas River Trail system is an 88-mile-long loop through the state which goes from the Clinton Presidential Bridge through North Little Rock and Big Dam Bridge, linking 38 Parks and six museums, and is used by cyclists, hikers, skaters, joggers, and walkers. Marion, Blytheville, Marked Tree, Bald Knob, Searcy, Beebe, Lonoke, and Arkadelphia are all towns in the region with exciting names. You may also want to visit Hot Springs near Fountain Lake.

Travelbest: I enjoyed a hike in the National Park and a 3.5-mile drive one way up the hill. I parked and strolled around the Tower for observation. Hot Springs Village had a little radio station warning listeners like me that the temperature was dropping six degrees in 30 minutes. Strong wind and rainfall followed. I had a bad case of poison ivy from this hike.

Do walk through Riverfront Park.
Don't get poison ivy in the State Park.

Jackson, Mississippi

Sleeping: Airbnb, hotel, camping, motel
Transportation: car, bus, train
Eating: fried chicken, fried okra, biscuits and gravy, collard greens, catfish, cornbread, butter cookies, pot roast, soul food, barbeque
Packing: t-shirts in summer, warmer layers in winter, jeans
Suggested: Aquarium in Gulfport, Delta Blues Museum, State Capitol, Eudora

Welty House & Garden, University of Mississippi

The University of Mississippi is the main attraction in Jackson. Walk the campus grounds and nearby neighborhoods. You can park on weekends or during school hours and explore. Football is a religion in this area, so be sure to see the sports stadium. Downtown Jackson is a square-shaped central neighborhood with many shops, the city hall, and a statue of William Faulkner, a writer from here.

Travelbest: I visited nearby Highway 61 and drove along the Blues Highway, stopping at the Gateway to the Blues Museum. It wasn't very authentic, but the effort was commendable. I stopped in Tunica, MS. If you are a fan, visit Indianola, the birthplace home of BB King.

Do visit Downtown Jackson, Mississippi
Don't forget to see Ole Miss (University of Mississippi)

Missouri

Sleeping: Airbnb, hotel, camping, motel
Transportation: car, bus, train, boat
Eating: St. Louis Pizza, toasted ravioli, butter cake, cheese curds, barbeque
Packing: layers, cold weather clothing, hot weather clothing, umbrella
Suggested: small towns, non-touristy outdoor hiking, Walmart, read Huck Finn, theater shows

Branson

See the Jubilee Review at the Grand Country Music Hall, home of the Baldknobbers, for some down-home entertainment. One tourist map has an ad for the Fantastic Caverns, a ride-through cave several miles from Branson. They have a trolley system to get around town. At the Branson King Hotel, I went to the pool and read my book for a while. Other places to visit are Dinosaur Canyon Golf, Sawmill, the World's Largest Toy Museum, IMAX, Butterfly Palace, Acrobats of China, and Welk Resort. However, the region is generally too touristy for my taste.

Hannibal

You can take a 5-hour drive from Branson through the mountainous rocky south and up to the northern cornfields. Missouri has small towns, local stores, and Walmart and Dollar Stores. The city of Hannibal is on the Mississippi River, and you may want to bring one of your favorite Tom Sawyer books by Mark Twain here to read. Walk around the city streets and surprise yourself with your adventures here.

Travelbest: At 6 pm, I drove into Hannibal looking for Becky Thatcher's home. I found Tom Sawyer's home first. At 6:30 pm, a live orchestra started playing outside the ice cream store. People brought folding chairs. There were about 30 guests and 30 people in the band. Those driving by inside their cars stared at the musicians as they drove past, and even some motorcyclists expressed their pleasure with the music. It was a pleasant sight, with both classical and American tunes. I drove by the Caves and campground and painted the picket fence by Becky's house.

Do paint the fence white at Becky Thatcher's house.
Don't miss the small-town flavors of Missouri's cities.

Minneapolis, Minnesota

Sleeping: hotel, Airbnb, resort, motel, cabin, lodge, teepee, bed and breakfast inn

Transportation: car, bus, boat, skyway downtown

Eating: tater tot hotdish, wild rice, polish sausage, pho, Swedish meatballs

Packing: jacket, boots, thermals in winter, layers

Suggested: Minnehaha Park, farmers' market, Mall of America

Minnesota has terrific indoor and outdoor activities. Here are a few suggestions of places to visit solo there:

- Superior National Forest and Boundary Waters Canoe Area Wilderness
- North Shore Scenic Drive
- Voyageurs National Park
- International Wolf Center
- Minnesota State Capitol Building
- Mall of America
- Split Rock Lighthouse State Park

Travelbest: I went to Coon Dam in the summer, but it was so hot I could not stand outside for a long time. It was interesting to see how the water level changes in the dam through the steps or locks.

Do walk around downtown Minneapolis.

Don't miss the giant mall, the Mall of America.

Sallisaw, Oklahoma

Sleeping: hotel, cabin, inn, Airbnb

Transportation: car, bus, boat

Eating: chicken fried steak, barbeque, Indian tacos, fried onion burgers, fried okra

Packing: jeans, boots

Suggested: route 66, college sports, art, history and science museums, women's softball, rodeos, lakes

Sallisaw, Oklahoma, has Daylight Donuts, established in 1954, with a drive-through window for convenience. Albert State College, Indian Tech Center, and Walmart are near Sallisaw, and you may enjoy visiting this area off the beaten path. The clay dirt is red in color. You may be surprised by the highway tolls, which add to the cost of auto travel. The payment request at the tolls continues throughout Oklahoma. Each stop was about $2.00 or $2.50. So, in all, about $10 in tolls. Tulsa had virtually no traffic, even during rush hour, which is good if you dislike traffic congestion.

Travelbest: When in Oklahoma, I visited small towns, such as Sallisaw, and saw a large cemetery right off the freeway. I parked at Daylight Donuts and stretched my legs. The next-door Valero gas station had two ladies counting coins at the register. They gave me a key with access to their restrooms. I walked around the parking lot, avoiding the puddles, and into the Donut store where the bathroom was. There was a lot of road construction while I was driving around Oklahoma. It was not a memorable place to visit.

Do visit some out-of-the-beaten-path locations.

Don't forget to eat barbecue.

North Dakota

Sleeping: hotel, ranch, inn, Airbnb, camping

Transportation: car, bus, train

Eating: walleye fish, hot beef sandwich, sauerkraut, knoephla soup, fleischkuekle meat pastry

Packing: layers, raingear

Suggested: Hjemkomst, Teddy Roosevelt National Park, and the National Buffalo Museum.

North Dakota may be the last US state which many people visit because it's not on the way to many other places. There was no distinct demarcation between the cities in the Moorhead/Fargo region of North Dakota. One could hardly tell where a city started or ended. The locals don't notice the change from one state to another. The river is the dividing line to enter North Dakota, but no sign in town announces arriving in a different state in the US. Painted Canyon Visitor Center should be a stop on your next trip to Fargo to get familiar with the region. As you would imagine, there is plenty of buffalo and camping here to enjoy. Visit the many parks, museums, and art galleries, and mix in with the locals. You will find four university campuses to walk around; North Dakota State University, University of Minnesota, Moorhead, and Concordia University are all within walking distance. In Fargo, visit the Hjemkomst (pronounced YEM-komst) Center, a scenic museum complex with a replica of a Norwegian Viking ship and a wooden stave church. The name means "Homecoming," which represents the Nordic people. The Plains Art Museum is one of the most visited places in Fargo. It is the largest art museum in North Dakota, with over 4,000 local, regional, and national works. If you are interested in local art, this is the place for you. Other popular sites in North Dakota are the Teddy Roosevelt National Park and the National Buffalo Museum.

Travelbest: I spent three days in Fargo, North Dakota. I considered flying there, but the flights were inconvenient as most of the towns in the area were small. Instead, I drove to Fargo, the largest city in the state, from Minneapolis, Minnesota. During the winter, I'd probably NOT travel here, but in the spring, summer, and fall, you may like this area since there are so few people and plenty of nature to enjoy. There was a storm with lightning, wind, hail, and TV warnings in nearby cities. After waking up in the bedroom after the storm, I was well-rested and relaxed. My Airbnb hostess, Alice, showed me a tree that fell on the neighbor's house. The mayor was around to inspect it. It could cost $10k to remove since there were six or seven main trees, and this one was dead.

Do explore the Hjemkomst Center.

Don't miss out on talking to the locals, who are mostly very friendly here.

South Dakota

Sleeping: hotel, motel, cabin, resort, Airbnb

Transportation: car, bus, bike

Eating: bierocks, pheasant, walleye, rocky mountain oysters, kolache, fudge

Packing: comfy shoes, layers, jeans

Suggested: Western South Dakota: Needles Highway, Custer State Park, Mount Rushmore Monument, Badlands, Wind Cave, Hot Springs

Eastern South Dakota: Falls Park, Harley Museum, Wall Drug, Corn Palace

Other: Sturgis, Custer State Park, Wind Cave, Badlands National Parks, and Hot Springs

Mount Rushmore

Mount Rushmore National Memorial is a massive sculpture, a rock-carved mountain, with human faces sixty feet tall; George Washington, Thomas Jefferson, Theodore Roosevelt, and Abraham Lincoln are featured. This was completed in 1941 by Gutzon Borglum and his son Lincoln, who directed the project. It takes about two hours to see the attraction, including interactive exhibits. Crazy Horse, another massive-scale mountainside project still under construction, is located 45 minutes away.

Travelbest: I would like to revisit Mt. Rushmore at sunset or in the evening to see a live musical concert. The town where the monument stands is full of touristy signage. I found that staying in Hot Springs was more authentic, even though it was a few miles to drive there.

Do spend some quality time at the memorial.
Don't get close to a buffalo. They are faster than they look.

Custer State Park

Custer State Park along the Needles Highway is perfect for solo traveling nature lovers. The rocks are gray and pointy, and the road can be steep. There is a tunnel with one-lane-only traffic, so cars alternate. Drive from the south for the best views. This drive was as scenic as Yosemite or Yellowstone, only much smaller in scope. You could also go fishing or hike at Custer State Park.

Travelbest: Due to road construction, I drove the long way there on my visit, which was a bit dangerous, 15 miles on non-paved roads, with no cars in either direction. There were lots of hills and valleys. I was alone for long stretches of road without cell service. I saw buffalo, and I stayed away. Many prairie dogs scurried into their holes to escape a storm. They are not dogs—they are small, furry, herbivorous rodents, but they have warning calls that sound like a dog's bark, hence their name. They were good companions, and I took some photos.

Do bring home a rock from your travels here.
Don't expect cell service all the time.

Hot Springs

There's hardly any traffic in Hot Springs, South Dakota. You will enjoy hiking or biking; you can also try to complete the Centennial Trail, 100 miles from start to finish. This trail goes from Deadwood, SD, south to Edgemont and follows the train tracks. You will observe prairie dogs and buffalo in the wild. Other places to see in this area are Jewel Cave, Freedom Trail, Cascade Falls, Mickelson Trail, Mammoth Cave and Dig, and Pioneer Museum. Mammoth Cave is an active working excavation site and has the fossils of over 60 mammoths. Reptile gardens and the Museum of Woodcarving are suggested attractions.

Travelbest: When I visited Wind Cave National Park, I met Mallory, the guide at the Visitor's Center, who helped me plan a solo 5-mile trek loop from Lookout Point to Centennial Trail. At the end of my hike, I saw a family of six, two adults and four young children, and I warned them of poison ivy since they were not wearing long sleeves and pants. Before this human encounter, it was only prairie dogs and me for the 5-mile hike. There was a lot of poison ivy;

thankfully, I wore long pants and hiking books for protection. I kept these dirty clothes in a closed bag in my trunk and washed my hands very often.

I visited Moccasin Springs Natural Mineral Spa in Hot Springs. It was very relaxing and refreshing. I spent hours soaking in the mineral pool (about 88 degrees Fahrenheit), talking with two women on a road trip and an older couple from Deadwood, South Dakota. These springs have been bubbling for over 129 years. Water is filtered through the earth, flowing into a natural red rock formation. Hot spring's natural water goes right into the pool. I got a sunburn, but it wasn't too bad. I would recommend this place. It's open from Wednesday to Sunday. I found that staying in a Hot Springs Airbnb was more authentic than a chain hotel, even though it was a few miles to drive there.

Do visit Moccasin Springs Spa in Hot Springs for a massage.

Don't get poison ivy infections.

Sturgis

The town of Sturgis is a motorcycle heaven. The annual August rally brings hundreds of thousands of bikers into town. The museum here is the Sturgis Motorcycle Museum and Hall of Fame. The bikers' slogan is "Honor the ride." The museum is a tribute to the people, the tradition, and the technology of motorcycles.

Lesson learned-My "shortcut" through South Dakota wasn't short.

The most efficient drive from Fargo to Sturgis would have been the interstate, but I took a left turn in Bismarck, North Dakota, and headed south to get a closer look at the land and people here. A few hours later, I saw a small sign with the words "locals only," but it was temporary, so I thought I'd try it. Twenty-five miles in, I was forced to turn around because the Sioux Indian tribe set up a checkpoint to keep outsiders away during Covid-19. I had to drive 50 extra miles, which added more time to a long drive. Don't try to drive through an Indian reservation when it is for residents only. You'll arrive at your destination sooner if you heed signage like this.

Wall

Have you seen Wall Drug? It's in the town named Wall. Since 1931, the drugstore has offered free ice water to attract tourists. The drugstore has grown into a commercial enterprise the size of 20 shopping malls. Here you can find Black Hills Gold, an art gallery, a dining hall, a café, a saloon, and rock/fossil shops—with plenty of western wear such as boots and hats. You will see multiple signs advertising the store for hundreds of miles before you arrive.

Mitchell

In the small city of Mitchell, you will find a tourist attraction called the Corn Palace that some tourists consider a don't-miss attraction. It is an exhibition space downtown with uniquely designed corn murals. Hundreds of thousands of tourists troop in yearly, although there is not much to see.

Sioux Falls

What can you do in Sioux Falls? A downtown Sculpture Walk is perfect for early morning strolls. You could stop by some retail stores such as the Duluth Trading Co store. While you're there, read a book on how they built the brand and retail chain. There are a few other friendly stores in the downtown area. Notice the old brick buildings which have been restored to their original architecture. There is traffic on the busy sidewalks and many tourist shopping options. You could also drive to the Great Plains Zoo, about 10 minutes away and worth a visit.

The Big Sioux River tumbles over a series of rock faces in Falls Park, which includes an observation tower and the ruins of the 19th-century Queen Bee Mill. Take the elevator to the top deck and get a 360-degree view of the city. The breeze will be refreshing as well. Then see the waterfalls downstairs. This is one of the visual highlights of the city; it's in an accessible and easy-to-find city park.

Travelbest: Summer temperatures rose above 90 degrees (Fahrenheit), but it felt more like 100 degrees due to the humidity. I used my umbrella for shade, which helped reduce the sun's heat on me. From there, I headed to Ike's Place in Tea, South Dakota, for relaxation and writing at his quiet Airbnb.

Do visit Falls Park and the observation tower.

Don't miss the downtown retail shopping.

Wichita, Kansas

Sleeping: hotel, Airbnb, motel

Transportation: car, bus, bike

Eating: barbeque, pizza, steak, ribs, Kansas dirt cake, bierocks, lefse, Corned beef and cabbage

Packing: denim jeans, light jacket, warm clothes in winter, rain gear

Suggested: Old Cowtown Museum, Keeper of the Plains, Great Plains Nature Center, Sedgwick County Zoo, Wichita Art Museum

Think of sunflowers, wheat, midway, and a central location of the USA. Your first solo travel stop should be downtown Wichita, Kansas. Keeper of the Plains is an outdoor monument to the natives and their culture. It is a bridge surrounded by nature and several museums and parks. You must see this in person to experience it because a photo can't describe the atmosphere. There's even a troll here if you want to learn about local legends. Hint: It's a statue. Nearby, you can park and walk to Exploration Place, a hands-on science museum on the Arkansas River. During the summer months, wear bug repellant as there are several flying insects. The Wichita Art Museum was a nice change of pace with a very reasonable admission fee. The Sedgwick County Zoo may be your favorite part of Wichita, including a mini tropical forest, birds, reptiles, penguins, and elephants. The Old Cowtown Museum is a delightful surprise, especially friendly to veterans and travelers with a sense of history.

Travelbest: I took a short tour of "Exploration Place," but most exhibits did not interest me. The Great Plains Nature Center was delightful, and I hiked the area.

Do visit the Wichita Art Museum and Sedgwick County Zoo.

Don't miss the sculpture in the downtown area called "Keeper of the Plains," as it is a treasure.

Western USA

California (East to West)

Sleeping: hotel, motel, Airbnb, resort

Transportation: car, bus, train, golf carts

Eating: Fish tacos, In-N-Out Burger, carne asada burrito, sushi, almonds, avocados, grapes, steak, walnuts

Packing: Jeans, sneakers, life jacket, layers, rain gear, umbrella

Suggested: Disneyland, California Adventure, wineries, Catalina Island, boardwalk

Note: Lake Tahoe is presented in Nevada, which follows next.

Catalina Island

Most people go to the town of Avalon. It's a small town, mostly toured with golf carts. Take the high-speed boat from Long Beach and visit the island; a one-day or weekend trip is good. It takes only one hour via high-speed ferry or

15 minutes via helicopter to get you to this island paradise. Two companies offer ferry service from the Southern California cities of Long Beach, San Pedro, Dana Point, and Newport Beach to Avalon and Two Harbors. There is a Wrigley Family (chewing gum) history to discover when you arrive. Rent a golf cart or a bicycle when you arrive. They rent by the hour.

There are still wild bison on this island. If the ocean is rough, be sure you take your seasick medication in advance of boarding.

Travelbest: The first time here, I went to Twin Harbors, camped, and discovered beautiful natural scenery and lovely places for swimming. I've enjoyed staying in town, too.

Do rent a golf cart or bicycle.
Don't get seasick on the ferry ride.

Pacific Beach

Pacific Beach (PB) is a neighborhood of roughly 50,000 people living near the ocean, including youthful sports activities like biking and swimming. Residents enjoy sunshine, nightlife, the ocean boardwalk, and the bayside near Mission Boulevard, Garnet, and Grand Avenues. What should you do in PB? First, orient yourself to the cement boardwalk and walk the ocean and bayside. Afterward, get a bike and ride along the flat areas to see other neighborhoods. Take a stroll in the afternoon and soak in the sounds, the smells, and the local culture. Unhoused pepoe live on the streets here, like in every major city. There are trendy hotels and bars. You'll see churches and stores, along with other things to do for entertainment, plus a wide selection of restaurants and cafes.

Travelbest: I've lived in San Diego for decades and lived in the PB area for a few of those years. I was married in a church in a neighborhood here. I've stayed here for three staycations in the past few years at the Crystal Pier Cottages, which are a delightful experience, especially in fall or spring. I lived in a home on the boardwalk, so I recommend getting familiar with this area for a colorful slice of life in Southern California. This is a good Step 2 destination if you prefer a temperate climate and like the casual beach lifestyle.

Disneyland, Anaheim

Here's what you need for a fun Step 1 or 2 solo Disneyland experience. Most days are very crowded here with long lines, so to maximize your time, you need to plan your trip well, especially for the rides for which a FastPass is recommended. First, get a map of the park and parking lots, and download the app. The app provides accurate waiting times for rides. Second, check the calendar and scheduled open/close times to find the busy and blackout days and avoid them. For example, don't go on weekends or in summer if you can avoid it. Christmas at Disneyland is a treat because families are all around, so the spirit is joyful and respectful. Halloween is spooky, and the rides are "dressed" up. Are the new Star Wars rides worth it? If you are a Star Wars fan—yes, they are. If you're not a fan, enjoy the park early on the other rides first. The Resistance Ride requires you to sign up for a "group" immediately after you enter the park. Not everyone will get on this ride. There are a limited number of groups guaranteed to get in each day.

For some rides, like the new Star Wars ride, you can ride "single" as a solo traveler and save time. This is a winning part of solo travel. Some of the rides had a wait of 75 to 90 minutes, and solo riders are used to fill in empty seats to maximize ridership.

- It's a Small World is a traveler's pleasure ride. It's fun for anyone who likes to see different cultures, and the music is easy to sing. If you've never been on this ride, go there first. It was first introduced at the New York World's Fair in 1964.
- Nemo: You'll be underwater in a submarine with views of sea life. You will like the 3-D images of the scuba divers and fish in Disney style. If you are claustrophobic, skip this one. It's for the non-disabled only. There is no single rider line here. Sit on tiny seats and look through a porthole.
- Pirates of the Caribbean is always a recommended ride on the water.
- Jungle Cruise is good if you want to have some silly laughs.
- Tom Sawyer Island has outdoor activities like walking over bridges and caves.
- Train Ride around the park. One of my favorite rides. Get on/off when you see something you like. It makes several stops and goes through some exhibits, too.

The long lines for food can be an opportunity. Look up the rules on what you can bring into the park to eat. You will find tasty meals in Fantasyland at the River Belle Terrace. Stay for the evening events if you can. The fireworks make for a beautiful finale to a happy day. You can stay after the fireworks for a few last rides and shop before the park closes to miss the crowds leaving at the same time. Check the Disneyland app to find the daily schedules and prepare to wait in long lines.

Travelbest: My favorite days to go to Disneyland are birthdays, even if it's summertime crowded, because the guest gets a unique Disney Birthday pin to wear. Rainy days are also less busy, in my experience, but there are few of those in the summer. I had trout in Fantasyland for lunch, which was good, with excellent service. Plan your trip. I was introduced to It's a Small World exhibit at the New York World's Fair in 1964, and I've loved it since then.

Disneyland: California Adventure, Anaheim

This park ranks second best in the area, just across the plaza from the first, Disneyland. You may be able to get a park-hopper ticket for an extra fee. You should download the app and get to know the geography because you'll be doing much walking these days. Be sure to have comfy shoes and a positive attitude regarding crowds. Parking is expensive at Disney theme parks. If you're staying at a nearby hotel, use rideshare, and you'll save cash. I parked about 2 miles away and took the rideshare, with a fee under $10. Plus, there were no lines to get on the bus to the parking area.

California Adventure is newer and has more attractions for adults than Disneyland. Like Disneyland, you can get one FastPass every two hours. You can also buy a MaxPass; these passes allow you to go to the front of the line with limitations and restrictions. Experts in Disney parks have studied this to provide successful outings. The more time you invest upfront in knowing your options, the better your in-park experience will be.

What are the best rides in California Adventure? "Soarin' over California" takes your chair on a ride, flying in a warehouse with a large video screen and viewing delightful locations that inspire travel. It is immersive and dark, and it stimulates all your senses. The ride is unforgettable if you like experiential travel. You'll be going further than you imagined. It's almost like you can feel the destinations, smell the food, and feel the wind rush past you. It was too short, but it was a great ride.

Getting around is easier if you use mobile technology, such as the Disneyland/California Adventure app. It provides information on the wait length, so you can judge if it's worth going there. Alcohol seems to be served in a dozen locations throughout the park. They even have a Sonoma-themed restaurant and winery on a small scale. You will love the Redwoods and the Boudin Bakery tour, with bread samples. The Incredibles roller coaster could get you dizzy. For food, the highlight is the Chicken Tenders Western Roundup restaurant near Soarin' over California. For snacks, you may bring several Ziplocs of trail mix, fresh fruits, and a water bottle to refill all day.

Travelbest: I attended a gospel music competition that was all-black and soulful. It was indoors, at a theater, in the section generally used to showcase the movie "Frozen." This experience can be a good respite if you want to be inside and with air conditioning in the summer. Due to the long line, I did not ride the Guardians of the Galaxy.

Napa Valley

Consider a visit to Napa Valley, California. Some wineries have regular hours, and others are open by appointment only. I went on a Saturday, so I'd advise you to get going early in the day if you travel on weekends. The earlier in the day you get to Napa and the region, the fewer the crowds and the traffic. If you plan your trip well, you should enjoy it more. Exploring new wine regions like Napa Valley can be the perfect trip and doesn't require much travel planning. I recommend Sutter Home Winery as your first and Berringer as your last stop. You can have a wonderful picnic lunch in between. Visit a grocery store before visiting the region and pick up a picnic lunch. You could also stop at the Oakville Grocery nearby, where you will find some of your favorite items like bread and cheese. Get some fresh fruit and healthy snacks, and plenty of non-alcoholic drinks.

Don't miss the famous Castle Diamorosa. I suggest you take a long look at the wine region map before you visit. There are 16 different districts where you will find several wineries. What will you be tasting? It'll most likely be Cabernet Sauvignon and Chardonnay since they are the most popular and grow best in this region. Napa Valley holds many surprises for wine lovers and beginners looking for flavors off the beaten path. There are more than three dozen different wine grape varieties in Napa Valley.

Someone responsible can be the designated driver who sticks to non-alcoholic drinks. You don't need to drink alcohol to have a great time. There are plenty of other things to do. You may also hire a car with a driver for the day; many people do this. Depending on your budget, you can make this a destination for your small group or yourself. You can also take rideshare between wineries, which will cost you between $10 to $30 each, depending on the distance. You can't walk from one winery to the other because there are no paths or sidewalks, and the area is not set up for this unless you are in the more urban downtown area of Napa.

Travelbest: On another previous trip, I visited Napa on the day of an earthquake. I knew the area had a 6.0 quake at 3 a.m., but I drove there anyway. Silver Oak Winery was hit, but they recovered very quickly. When I arrived a few hours later, the winery had cleaned up much of the debris, and they could give tours. To the casual observer, it was almost as though nothing significant had happened that day, even though they lost millions in damaged wine and materials.

Do enjoy some fresh outdoor wineries in Napa.
Don't forget to drink plenty of water and hydrate.

Big Bear Lake and Mountain

If you are in the Southern California region, one of the visits to the mountains should include Big Bear Lake. It's a city on the bank of the lake, known for Bear Mountain and Snow Summit ski resorts. There are terrain parks and learner slopes at each resort, and Bear Mountain tends to have more snowboarders at the terrain parks. The city is filled with village streets in a commercial area, including restaurants, gift shops, and small stores for groceries and other items. The San Bernardino National Forest surrounds the city. A single lift ticket is usable at Bear Mountain and Snow Summit. Even if you don't ski, you can still enjoy a day at the resort, snuggle up with a cup of cocoa and a good book to make your day cozy, and walk through some of the mountain areas safely with guidance from experts. The ski areas are a few hours' drive from Los Angeles or San Diego, and skiing starts in November until the snow melts, usually in April. Get here early or come for night skiing if you prefer.

You can ski here in winter and go boating in summer for decades. For example, you can book a sunset cruise on the larger boat, Miss Liberty. Or you can go on the Queen, a cruise with up to 60 passengers from May to October. It's a 90-minute excursion, narrated by the captain, who tells you about the area's history and shows you the highlights, best fishing spots, solar observatories, and celebrity homes.

In summer, you can take the chairlift up to the top of the mountain and hike or bike down, depending on your abilities. There is also the option to hike up part way and take the chairlift down. If you do hike, be sure to have sturdy hiking boots. Plenty of sunscreen lotion is also needed here.

Travelbest: One of my favorite things about Big Bear is hiking and the restaurants after the exercise. I recommend renting skis in the village, so you don't have to wait in long lines at the lodge.

Do go summer boating as it is beautiful.

Don't ski on weekends or holiday weekends as it's crowded.

Lesson learned - Not wearing proper hiking footwear

While hiking at Big Bear Mountain, we made our way down the mountain on foot from the top of the lift. Unfortunately, one of the women in my group had slipped and slid down several feet, causing a nasty rug burn and rash on her leg. It was also filled with dirt, so it was not easy to clean the wound. It took several months before all the scars from that wound healed. Be prepared for hiking in these circumstances. Wear the proper clothing, including pants and hiking boots, and be constantly aware of the terrain.

Lake Arrowhead Village

Lake Arrowhead is an outdoor paradise for those who enjoy nature and the beauty of mountains and forests. It's a privately owned lake and is restricted to use by homeowners and the resort's guests. The area around the lake's perimeter is Arrowhead Woods. You need permission to visit the lake if you're not staying at one of their properties. Locals are about 9,000 in population, so this small village swells in the summer months with tourism. Swimming is common here but check that it's allowed and safe before you swim. The most abundant fish you'll find in Lake Arrowhead are bass and trout. Crappie fishing is also getting more popular, as well as catfish. Be sure to bring your fishing license. There are many restaurants. Here are a few ideas of what to do in this area. You will see the resort from the lake, and you can walk around the nearby stores. There are plenty of attractions to visit, including Wildhaven Ranch, Mountain History Museum, Lake Gregory, Skypark at Santa's Village, and Heaps Peak Arboretum.

Travelbest: For my first wedding anniversary, my husband, three-month-old Catherine, and I explored Lake Arrowhead Village. I booked a tiny cabin not far from the resort. Since then, I have returned to this area many times to share the outdoors with my growing family. I learned a lot about fishing and hiking and had mountain adventures.

Do go on long mountain walks.

Don't swim by the shore in the lake without permission.

Redwoods of California

You will love the beauty of a Redwood forest, mentioned in the Woodie Guthrie song *This Land is Your Land*. "From the Redwood forest to the Gulf Stream waters, this land is made for you and me. This could be a Dr. Travelbest Step 1 or Step 2 travel destination, depending on your degree of adventure. If you love redwoods, this is the place for you. Be careful if you have a low-clearance vehicle or an RV, as that may be too big for some roads. The redwoods of California are near the coast, as opposed to sequoias, which are at a higher alpine elevation and inland. The redwoods are the tallest trees in the world. Coast redwoods live from 500 to 700 years, although some have been documented to live 2,000 years. The wood from these trees was a godsend for new home construction, decks, and other building materials. After World War II, many redwoods were cut down in California. Their thirst for fog and proximity to water sources could make their survival difficult with the current climate change. Warm air pulls moisture from the leaves, and trees close their pores to maintain their water supply. That prevents their intake of carbon dioxide and photosynthesis.

Want to visit the forest? There are no timed entries for Redwood National and State Parks, so come anytime, and plan to get the most out of your visit. Go to the visitor center first to get maps and talk to the rangers. Get off Highway 101 to explore redwood forests on foot, not just from your car. All trails are great, so ensure you get off the well-known areas and be mindful of nature. Think beyond Fern Canyon and Tall trees grove. Driving is tricky for larger RVs because the roads are windy, so ask the ranger if you have any concerns. Learn about traffic delays: your GPS will likely be wrong, so be prepared. Know what footwear you need.

Travelbest: Nearby, you can find Jedediah Smith Redwoods State Park (my favorite), Del Norte Coast Redwoods State Park, and Prairie Creek Redwoods State Park. I have often traveled along the coast to Crescent City, in northern California, and the Redwood Forest National Park is very close.

Do double the time you expect to spend driving; roads are slower and windy. Don't disturb the wildlife.

Nevada

Sleeping: hotel, casino, Airbnb, resort, ranch

Transportation: car, train, bus

Eating: Thai cuisine, shrimp cocktail, chicken wings, sushi, paella, casino buffets

Packing: Light jacket, hiking shoes or boots, sports equipment, layers

Suggested: Nature walks, ski resorts, Virginia City, Carson City, antique stores, snow, wild horses

Lake Tahoe, California, and Nevada

Lake Tahoe has three things: North Shore, near Highway 80 with mountains; ski resorts like NorthStar, brimming with beauty and elegance; and South Shore, with bustling tourism. If you drove around the lake and did not stop, it would take 3 hours. It is a total of 72 miles around.

The North Shore is quieter than the South Shore. It's got more nature and scenery, but fewer places to park. One thing to note is the beautiful, wild horses running nearby, especially along Highway 50, so be careful while driving. On the North Shore, you can cruise on a boat on the lake. Drive around the lake and spend a day just relaxing while you take in the scenery. For a taste of the Old West, visit nearby Virginia City.

The South Shore straddles both Nevada and California. The casinos are here. The Lake Tahoe Visitors Authority will help you find your way around the south part of the lake. There are plenty of places to stay and things to do here, including water sports and boating. It's geared for visitors, so go ahead and enjoy the beauty. About an hour from South Lake Tahoe, Virginia City offers you a step back to the 1800s. Ski resorts are big business in the winter here. My favorites are Heavenly Valley Resort, which covers two states; you can ski from California to Nevada and back.

Travelbest: I enjoyed the sunset dinner cruise to Zephyr Cove. Many boats were in the water, so it was not remote, but it was still lovely to visit.

Do visit Virginia City for the old west experience.
Don't lose much money at the casinos.

Reno

You can tour on a railroad which provides context to the many mining stories of yesteryear; the tour guide describes what life was like in the 1850s through 1890s when this was one of the largest silver mines in the world. The Comstock Lode of silver was the most significant find, making multiple millionaires of the prospectors lucky enough to stumble on this metal. Now, the lucky ones are the shopkeepers who sell their wares and make a few dollars in profit from the tourists. This small town has tourism as its only visible source of revenue.

Stay in the Reno hotels in the summertime and venture out for the day with drinks and coolers. Nothing is too expensive here except the gold and silver you may be tempted to take home. Winters are chilly, with skiing in the nearby mountains. You'll need to bring tire chains if you drive these mountains in winter. You will see beautiful scenery— June Lake, Yosemite, and Mono Lake— on your way to and from your destination. Reno and the Eastern Sierras may be your best bet if you are looking for a Western vacation spot close to other inexpensive travel destinations.

Travelbest: After a week in the Eastern Sierras, including Reno, Carson City, Virginia City, and Sparks, I headed home on Highway 15. The temperature was 96 degrees. I made two stops after leaving Sparks at 6:30 a.m. I stopped at Bishop for sandwiches at the famous Sheepherder's restaurant and then in Ridgecrest for gas. The trip's highlight was seeing my relatives and enjoying each other's company—a birthday party of 34 people from 10 regions of the US. The tourist activities were in Virginia City, where I visited the old schoolhouse and walked the sidewalks filled with authentic saloons and antique stores.

Do learn about the silver mining history.

Don't expect to find any gold.

3
ADVANCED SOLO TRAVEL STEP 3

Passports and immunizations may be required for Advanced Step 3 travel, along with international visas. This includes two US states: Hawaii and Alaska. You may also consider visiting foreign countries such as Canada and island nations in the Caribbean/Bahamas. In some areas, US passports, international visas, and international driving will be required. Your travel has advanced to the third and middle step in the 5 Steps to Solo Travel.

Alaska

Sleeping: Airbnb, hotel, motel
Transportation: car, bus, train, dog sled, electric bike
Eating: lingcod, salmon, flounder, seal liver, Eskimo potatoes, Eskimo ice cream, bear feet berries, fish, oysters, crab, reindeer sausage, Yak meat, fry bread
Packing: summer months bring bug repellent, t-shirts, shorts and raingear; winter climate requires a parka, boots, hat, gloves, or mittens
Suggested:

Denali National Park: Guided Tours of the park, glaciers, Iditarod dogs; Fairbanks: Howling Dog Saloon, Salmon Bake, Denali National Park, whale watching, glaciers, Farmers Market; Kenai area: including Seward and Homer, fishing, hiking, Land's End

Alaska is known as the 'Land of the Midnight Sun.' For Alaska, you will experience spring in June, summer in July, and fall in August. If you travel there in another month, you will be in winter weather, so consider going in July or August for the best weather and longest days, so you can do more while it's light outdoors. Alaska is a destination where you can find 3000 rivers, three million lakes, and 6640 miles of coastline. Most people and activities occur near the coastline, especially near Anchorage.

Denali National Park (formerly Mt McKinley)

If you're going to the park, consider the Summer Solstice, and hike at midnight. You can sit outside at 2 am, and it's still not dark. Inside the park, transportation is limited to basic school buses for your choice of tour length. Take the most extended tour to see as much of the park as possible on the bus, with multiple stops for rest and photo breaks. Savage River is the end where you can drive your car. The park was built in the 1920s and 1930s. Private vehicles belong only to park rangers or wildlife biologists (with a permit in the windshield that allows them in). The Denali campground is at mile 29 on the road and as far as you can drive to the Savage River. With reservations, you are permitted to drive your cars to the camp. It would be best if you stayed at least three nights, and you can only drive in on the first day and out on the last day.

If you are lucky, you join the '30% Club', which means you get to see the peak of Denali Mountain. Typically, the peak is not visible due to weather storms and clouds blocking the view. Only 30% of the people who visit from around the world get to see it. Glaciers are large carved valleys. It's a sub-arctic desert in Alaska, with an average of 30 inches of precipitation, like Tucson, Arizona. There is lots of rain at certain times of the year, so predictable rivers form. Alaskans are interested in protecting the tundra. Travelers should respect what the locals in Alaska want to preserve for future generations. In addition to Denali, look for the multicolored Polychrome Glacier, with volcanic rocks in colors of reds, oranges, grays, and blacks. Flowers and forests thrive in many Alaskan areas, and the landscape is green. You can walk around the kennels, check out the dogs that run the Iditarod sled race, and visit a small museum that displays some race memorabilia.

Lesson learned- Even in Alaska, you can sweat a lot.

I did not have air conditioning (AC) in Alaska, which was uncomfortable. That was hard to imagine. The temperature is normally pleasant in the summer, so the hotels don't all have AC. Ours didn't. We had a fan, and that helped.

Be prepared for any weather conditions.

Wildlife is wild. Don't approach animals. Stay at least 25 meters away, or two bus lengths. Human voices will keep animals away, most of the time. Here is how to handle the bears. Talk to others, make noise. If you see a grizzly bear, stay far, at least 300 yards/meters away. For distance comparison, think three football fields away. If you see a bear and if it does not know you are there, stay quiet and walk away. They may stand up on their hind legs for a good vantage if they see you. Talk to the bear in a friendly, calm loud manner. "Hey, bear, I'm human." Raise your arms and backpack above your head and make yourselves look big. Slowly back off and walk away in a different direction. Do not run from a grizzly bear. Stand your ground, as they can run 35 mph. You can't outrun them, so don't trigger the response. Stand your ground. Don't run. The last option is to play dead, so roll into a ball and protect your head with your arms. Even better is purchasing protection ahead of time. Buy bear spray and use it upwind. You have to be quite close to be effective in using it. Keep it tucked away in the middle of your backpack.

Don't overlook Alaska's most dangerous animal, the moose, which are 3-4 times larger than bears and unpredictable. If they are upset and charge at you, run away in a zigzag pattern. Moose are large and gangly. Mother moose who have calves are very protective of their young ones. Be safe and keep the animals far away from you. Tell a park ranger if you do have an encounter.

Kenai: Homer

I saw Homer, Alaska, on July 4 at 11:30 p.m. for the first time when the sky was still very bright. The fireworks were delightful, even though they were hard to see since it was nearly daylight all night long. It is a city in the Kenai Peninsula, 218 miles southwest of Anchorage, and a beautiful drive from that destination. Five thousand year-round residents include many people in fishing and tourism, with three intense months to earn hospitality income. This is the Halibut Capital of the World. Homer has scenic coastal views at the very end of Highway 5, which begins in San Diego, California. When you drive here, you feel like it's the end of a very long road, hence the name, Land's End.

Consider fishing and hiking in the area. Get ready for the state bird (the mosquito) to join the hike. Remember to protect your skin from other things like poison ivy. You can fish on open seas or smaller lakes and reservoirs in this area. Salmon fishing is challenging and worth attempting if you have never tried it.

The Division of Sport Fish allows for the sport fisheries protection, maintenance, and improvement. Where you begin fishing depends on your taste for river or ocean fishing. You must purchase a fishing license before heading out on the water. Know the day you will be fishing and the fish you will be catching because the license could be different depending on the day and region. The rules on what fish you can catch and the limit can change, so ask many questions here.

An excellent place to start fishing is to visit the area in person and get to know the boats arriving with plenty of fish. The best captains are those you like, so get to know some captains by hanging out at the dock and talking to informed people. You can cook the fish you caught at your local restaurant and eat them fresh. You can also freeze them and have them shipped on your plane or mail them.

Travelbest: I've been fishing in Alaska since 1993 and have been lucky to catch 125 lb. halibut, several rockfish, and more. I enjoyed my Alaska solo travels outdoors because it's a unique territory and landscape. You could catch enough halibut to pay for your trip like I did—twice! Once in '94 and again in 2019. Hiking in Alaska makes me smile.

Do prepare for any weather.
Don't forget to purchase your fishing license, or you will be fined.

Kenai: Seward

Tourism is the primary industry for Seward, AK, where the population swells from 3,000 in the winter to 30,000 in the summer. This city is an inlet on the Kenai Peninsula with fjords, penguins, whales, mountains, and hiking trails. If you love whale watching, you'll be interested in watching the gray whale mating ritual from the shore or on a boat. You should also see the glaciers. Yes, they are melting fast, so this may be one of the last chances you have to experience this phenomenon. I had some slowdowns due to fires, so plan for these waits during summer.

Seward is a fishing town. The library and town hall are in the same building. Downtown is easy to find and walkable. There're a few museums and shops to see, but most of what you will enjoy is the outdoors. Alaska's Sea Life Center was overpriced for what you see, so unless you have free passes, skip it. There's plenty of outdoors to see instead. My favorite parts of Seward are hiking trails, rainbow vistas, deep-sea fishing, and ocean views.

Travelbest: I was there in '94 and returned 25 years later. I can tell you climate change is dramatic. I recommend you fly to Anchorage and drive to Seward.

Rent a spot on a boat for a day and fish your heart out. I had some traffic stops and slowdowns due to fires, so plan for these waits during summer.

Do rent a boat for a day and bring seasick meds.

Don't let a rainy day pass you by. Pick some indoor activities and enjoy them. Alaska's Sea Life Center was not worth the money.

Fairbanks

Fairbanks, Alaska, known as the Golden Heart City, has a lot to offer in the summer. It is known for bike trips, log cabins, and flightseeing, where you can design your travel experience in the sky. They even have semi-professional baseball teams which play at midnight without artificial lights. The weather can be a pleasant 70 degrees in the summer. Look for Outdoor art, murals, and wildlife scenes. The most commercial location was the Pioneers Park of Alaska Museum. This is a big, nearly empty touristy spot. Salmon Bake is a world-class dinner in the park, and it's open daily.

We visited the city called the North Pole, went to the store, met with Santa Claus, and shopped for Christmas decorations. The town has candy cane-striped streetlights. The walls of the store are covered with children's letters to Santa. The streets are named Kris Kringle Drive and Mistletoe Lane.

Visit the Howling Dog Saloon if you want to meet some residents of Fairbanks. They had a live concert and fundraising for a local charity the day we were here. We met the owner and had a great visit. The Silver Gulch is across the street for a finer dining establishment and, notably, a Triple D on Guy Fieri's list of great places to eat.

Travelbest: I also spent an afternoon in the hot springs near China River and

Chena Lake Recreation Area and hiked a few of the nature trails. It was unusually boiling and muggy that summer and our hotel did not have air conditioning.

Do eat at the Salmon Bake in Fairbanks at Pioneers Park.
Don't get too close to a moose.

Ship your Alaskan frozen fish

Explore some of the ways fish are frozen and shipped back home. Before you get on your fishing boat, know what you want to do with your catch and how much you want to bring home. You may pay an extra fee to ship your boxes of frozen fish on the plane. Be sure you get fish frozen and professionally packed for the airplane, as it's cheaper than mailing it to yourself.

Travelbest: I went fishing in Alaska and had a local company freeze and pack 187 lbs. of fish for $400. I paid the excess airline baggage fees, which were $200 for four large boxes. However, this was much less expensive than shipping via FedEx, as I shipped 50 pounds for about $150. Overall, this method of fishing almost paid for my entire two-week trip, considering if I was to purchase at the retail cost of the fish. I've been fishing in Alaska since 1993 and have been lucky to catch 125 lb. halibut, several rockfish, and more.

Do prepare for any weather.
Don't forget to purchase your fishing license, or you will be fined.

Lesson learned- Getting soaked and frozen while fishing in Alaska

Fishing began at 6 am, and we caught one fish at 6:05 am. We were invigorated and triumphant at this good fortune. We had not expected to catch a fish so fast. This emotion slowly seeped away as the day dragged on without a bite. We caught no fish the rest of the day and finished at 1 pm, soaking wet and miserable. Dress appropriately for a rain shower.

Hawaii

Sleeping: Airbnb, hotel, motel, hammock, beach napping

Transportation: Car, bus, train, electric bike

Eating: poke, Maui onions, pineapple, shave ice, awa, spam musubi

Packing: bathing suit, sandals, walking shoes, sunscreen

Suggested: Diamond Head, snorkeling, beach, Pearl Harbor, shopping, Polynesian Cultural Center, volcano tours at night, parasailing

Hawaii became a state in 1959, so it is still one of the newest regions of the USA. To get an overview of Hawaii, think of island life and how most people live near the coast, as in other parts of the world. These mountainous paradise-like islands are primarily tropical and rainy, growing lush with plants. Inland you will find different types of activities, depending on the island. Some islands are more populated, such as Oahu, where Honolulu is located. Others are less popular and attract tourists who want a more laid-back experience. Here I will describe Honolulu and the Big Island and what you can expect to do there as a solo traveler in Step 3.

Honolulu

On the island of Oahu is Honolulu, with stunning beaches with aquamarine colors and surf crashing on the rocks. There are artificial lagoons, like the Marriott's Ko Olina, or rugged, relatively undeveloped beaches, like Yokohama Bay, with white sand and warm turquoise water. Oahu's beaches are in one of four locations with over 100 miles of shoreline. Here is a summary of the four: North, South, West, and East.

The famous North Shore has surfing beaches, like Waimea Bay and Ehukai Beach, home of the Banzai Pipeline. These are popular with expert surfers worldwide.

The South Shore is for Waikiki and city beaches, and fun snorkeling. Bring or rent your fins, mask, and snorkel and head into the water. Tall palm trees and luxury resort hotels border these vast, wide beaches. The Westside's beaches are Leeward Coast, which means they are protected from the wind by the island. This is where you'll find peaceful beaches with gentle surf, like Ko Olina and Turtle Bay.

On the Eastside, referred to as the Windward Coast, you'll find famous yet unspoiled beaches, like Waimanalo and Makapuu. Some days you will find rainy, windy areas along the beach and rocky shores. Some of the most popular beaches are on the East shores. East shore's Kailua is a swimming area with easy parking in the morning. It's a local beach with lifeguards, sports, and sailing. A favorite local beach is Lanikai Beach because it delivers all the elements: isolated yet accessible, near the town of Kailua on the Windward Coast. The beach is in a residential neighborhood, which keeps the crowds away but can create parking problems, so arrive early if possible. Lanikai has a full range of water sports, both on top of and under the water. You can sail, windsurf, sea kayak, and snorkel. Kayakers can even paddle out to tiny uninhabited islands about a mile offshore. The water is warm, clear, and gentle. An offshore reef protects it, and the sand is white and fine.

Kailua Beach Park is only a mile from Lanikai Beach and is constantly ranked as one of <u>America's best beaches</u>. You find three miles of white sandy beach with warm, gentle, greenish-blue water. The beach is part of a 35-acre park with all kinds of outdoor sports and recreation facilities. There is nearby dining in Kailua, including a shaved ice place called Island Snow. Shaved ice is famous here and is made from ground ice shavings, sweet syrup, and condiments served like ice cream in a cup.

Makapuu Beach

This beach is only 30 minutes outside Waikiki and delivers epic sunrise views, lots of remarkable lava rocks for picturesque backgrounds, and some great waves. The beach is especially famous for body surfing, and the waves are consistently sound. The water is dangerous, and there can be strong rip currents, so this spot is best for expert body surfers. It's for body surfing only - no surfboards are permitted here.

The beach is next to Makapuu Point, the eastward part of Oahu. There's a lighthouse on the point and some cool sea caves in the rocks beneath it. The 1,000-foot-long beach is bright white with powder-soft sand. The white sand creates an image that gives the water a light turquoise color. The beach is broader during summer, and the sand erodes due to winter waves. After enjoying the beach, I recommend you hike along the adjacent Point Lighthouse Trail. The walk is about three miles round-trip to and from the lighthouse and provides some seriously jaw-dropping ocean views.

Waimea Bay is a famous surfing spot, and the beach here is always a great place to visit, even for non-surfers. With all the surfers, there's always something to see. The monster waves Waimea is famous for only occur during the winter; the surf is gentle during the summer, making it great for swimming and snorkeling. During the winter, the beach can experience waves as high as 20 to 30 feet, some of the largest in the world. Waimea Bay has good facilities, public restrooms, outdoor showers, and lifeguards. The sand is powder smooth, and the beach is wide. After a day of water sports, get a bite with the locals at one of the many food trucks that line the Kamehameha Highway near all the famous surf breaks.

Waikiki

The best time to visit Waikiki is early Sunday morning due to light auto traffic. Las Vegas-type mega hotels such as Iliki, Hilton Hawaii Village, etc., are in this area, with shops reminding me of Beverly Hills retail, including Harry Winston, Gucci, and Coach. Swimming can sometimes be dangerous as Catamaran sailboats land on the shore. They beep their boat horns as they approach the beach to tell the swimmers like me to get out of the way.

Go snorkeling in the Waikiki area at Sans Souci Beach or Queens Beach. Bring a facemask, snorkel, and fins. See plenty of coral and fish that are translucent, jelly-like, and polka-dotted. Colorful plants are in abundance by the aquarium. I met up with the Women's Synchronized Swimming team from the University of California, Berkeley, practicing here early Sunday morning as I went snorkeling solo.

If you are not a beach traveler, you can visit the following:

1) The Bishop Museum includes five buildings including a Planetarium and interactive exhibits.

2) Diamond Head crater hiking. Walk through the tunnel, which is part of a crater. Picnic spot by the parking lot. Park by the community college nearby if you can't find a parking spot.

3) Pearl Harbor Museum USS Arizona, a 3-minute walk from USS Bowfin Sub Museum. Make your reservations well in advance and be prepared to wait in lines. The slogans include: "Remember Honor Understand." Visit the USS Missouri Battleship, used through '99, built in 1944.

4) Polynesian Cultural Center in the northeast part of the island has a beautiful setup, so get your tickets in advance. The buffet, the evening show, and the experience are one of a kind. You will feel the Hawaiian culture more than other places on the islands. It's for tourists and may be worth it if you have a car, as it's a one-hour drive from the main parts of the island.

5) Shopping. The downtown Waikiki mall has free parking and 400+ stores, plus a food court. You can walk to the beach from here, too. If you are looking for some Hawaiian food, try this. Mana musubi is a snack of rice and nori, a seaweed wrap with Spam inside. Spam is prevalent in Hawaii.

Lesson Learned- Not taking responsibility for my actions

We all need to be better at taking responsibility for our actions. In my younger years, I often was guilty of wasteful activities and littering from my car window.

Kuleana has this meaning: "Responsibility." I also learned the following: "Take wisdom, make it deep. Be good to nature. Respect the land."

Hawaii's Big Island

The southern spot in the US is the southern tip of the Big Island. Have you seen the TV show Hawaii 5-0? What about Lost, the TV series? There are many shows and films made here. Scenic is an understatement.

The Big Island has much volcanic activity. You can walk across the lava at night and learn about the history and culture of the families that have lived on this land for hundreds of years. Many of them lost their homes due to the lava flows. If you have the opportunity, take a nighttime walking lava tour near Hilo. Due to these lava flows, the landscape could change with every visit. Island Insiders know the best sunrise views. You can take a helicopter tour or a zipline experience if you wish. Driving around the island is almost essential; you will need to rent a car to see most of this island, especially non-touristy places. Marine tourism is massive in Hawaii. Sixty percent of marine animals can't be seen anywhere else in the world. Get up close and personal with snorkeling or scuba diving. You may need to drive a bit to find what you want, including shark swimming. You will often see spinner dolphins, sea turtles, and endangered Hawaiian monk seals. Be relaxed when swimming with sharks, hammerheads, and more. They are revered in Hawaiian culture.

Parasailing in Hawaii brings you about 20 stories up, and it is a thrill to be pulled by a boat and then brought back to the ship. Have someone on the boat take your photo for free instead of the official photographer. Do it if you can for some outstanding views and memories. Make your reservation upon arrival, and then show up for a fun adventure. You will need to sign a health waiver for this activity.

Travelbest: My first visit to Hawaii was in 1982, and I never left the airport as I was only going through immigration and customs from the South Pacific, and there was no time. I was moving to San Diego, so I thought I'd be there often. It was finally in 2018 that I returned, and again in 2020. In 2018, I stayed in Kona, on the island's west side, and drove my rental car to the southernmost point of the USA and then to the eastern area of Hilo. From there, I went to the Mauna Loa and Mauna Kea Volcano areas, where I saw snow at the peak. I walked across the lava at night and learned about the history and culture of the families that have lived on this land for hundreds of years. Several volcanoes a few months after my visit changed the scenery dramatically.

Do find a hidden place in Hawaii. You can explore and discover many to call your own.

Don't go too close to the lava because it is unsafe.

Canada

Sleeping: hotel, Airbnb

Transportation: Car, train, bus

Eating: cheese, crispy crunch, poutine, Shritzlach, smoked meats, meat pie, Prince of Wales Hotel Afternoon Tea, Royal Stewart Dining Room

Packing: cold weather protection in winter, light clothing in summer

Suggested: Canadian National Parks, Banff Springs Hotel, Sulfur Mountain Trail, Lake Louise Chateau, IceFields Highway, Whistler gondola, Butchart Gardens, Prince of Wales Hotel Afternoon Tea, Royal Stewart Dining Room

Canada is the easiest to navigate if you want to drive. You can cross the border in several places near US cities. You may be crossing into Canada from Washington State, Montana, Michigan, New York, or a New England state.

You may be flying into these Canadian airports for your trip, the most well-known being Toronto, Montreal, and Vancouver. You will need your passport for Canadian travel. Ensure you follow the travel restrictions, if any, as they may have changed. To prepare, visit the websites for Canadian travel for passport holders from your country. Roaming is a challenge using mobile phones. Ex: Bell Canada phone line is more expensive. Canada has high data and high mobile costs. ATT and T-Mobile are cheaper and allow for roaming.

Banff

Six mountain ranges meet here at the view from Sulphur Mountain. Take your breath away vistas can be seen 360 degrees. The gondola cabin whisks you to the top, where you seem to fly over the Rocky Mountains trees. The elevation is 7500 ft (2281 meters). You can visit the restaurants, exhibits, theater, and observation deck along the ridge above. You can also hike the mountain and take the gondola down if you crave strenuous exercise.

Lake Louise Resort may be on your travel "bucket list" destination. You will want to visit the Banff Springs Hotel (Fairmont) for the best tea/coffee ever. Drive to the Lake Louise Chateau (Fairmount) and have one of the best buffet breakfasts. It is five-star quality and has a high price to match, but you can eat a large meal that lasts for the day. The weather may be pouring rain, then sunny skies within an hour, and the beauty can be seen in the reflective turquoise water. Nearby is the Ice Fields Highway. 3-5 hours to a full-day drive, depending on how often you stop to admire the scenery. One more recommendation is the breakfast at the Prince of Wales (Prince Albert Hotel) will be worth the extra time and expense.

Consider buying the Canadian National Park annual pass if you visit several parks. The senior discount is suitable for two people per vehicle, so it's better to go for the yearly family pass if you have more passengers. A single park pass gets you to all national parks, national historic sites, and national marine conservation areas operated by Parks Canada. The Discovery Pass provides unlimited admission for an entire year at over 80 parks, typically charging a daily entrance fee, plus you can skip the long line. I drove north to Jasper, Canada, and then headed west. The stunning Canadian Icefields Highway is nearby. It will take 3-5 hours to complete a full-day drive, depending on how often you stop to admire the ice fields.

Travelbest: Many Glaciers Hotel (This is the name, Many.) was delightful to enjoy for the evening, but unfortunately I could not stay the night since I did not have a reservation. I found a nearby hotel, which was sufficient. I drove to Banff, to the Canadian Rockies, and took a strenuous hike to the top of the Sulfur Mountain Trail, a distance of 3.4 miles and a half mile elevation gain (2.5-3 hours). Here, I saw stunning views of the Bow Valley. I followed a short trail up to the historic Cosmic Ray Station. After this strenuous hike, my hotel's heated pool at the bottom of the mountain felt great. Banff is known for hot springs, and I can confirm it was delightful.

Do a hike in Banff and enjoy the mountain air and hot springs.
Don't miss seeing Lake Louise and the Banff Springs Hotel.

Whistler

Whistler is the home of the Sasquatch, also known as Bigfoot. If you're driving, this is a long road trip across Canada, from Glacier National Park to Banff and Jasper and then from Whistler to Vancouver. This mountain town resort has much to do, especially if you like outdoor sports. Skiing and mountain biking are prevalent. There's also whitewater rafting, ziplining, helicopter rides, golf, and more. You will also enjoy shopping and eating in the downtown village by the Whistler Gondola, enjoying the views from a low altitude. You have both Blackcomb and Whistler mountains, plenty of hotels and lodges, and the Olympic Plaza. It's 75 miles (125 km) to Vancouver and one of the most scenic drives in the world.

Do visit the Olympic village.
Don't miss out on the sports and the views in the area.

Vancouver

This city is a bustling west coast seaport in British Columbia and one of Canada's most ethnically diverse cities. Hollywood uses the background as a location for filming movies because mountains surround it. The city of Vancouver has an artistic vibe as well. The traffic lights were blinking green, which meant advance go. That person has the right of way above everyone else. I found a nice neighborhood called White Rock. It's a few miles out of the main town and relaxing. The HOV lanes are on the right instead of on the left, as they are in the US. This is an example of different perspectives on different country traffic pattern needs. The World's Fair in 1986 was a special event for the people of Vancouver. Even though that was nearly 40 years ago, many locals remember how this transformed their city. When you visit, ask senior residents about the World's Fair. They will be delighted to tell you about their experiences. Many Canadians travel because of their long winter. Visit Victoria and Butchart Gardens as well as the wilds of the island. I'd highly recommend that if you can. These are maybe the loveliest gardens in the world.

Travelbest: I drove to Vancouver from Whistler, one of the most scenic drives in the world. I arrived without a plan for where to go or what to do, and I ended up on Granville Island and found the Public Market. You will love this market if you like seeing fresh fish, veggies, fruits, and local colors. It felt like I was surrounded by water. I stopped for lunch at a local seafood restaurant and watched the paddleboards and ferries pass by. My dear Canadian friend Heather Kingston is originally from Vancouver and is a world traveler like you will be someday.

Do see the Butchart Gardens for a lovely day among flowers.
Don't stop on blinking green lights. That means advanced go, and you have the right of way.

British Virgin Islands

Sleeping: Hotel, Airbnb

Transportation: Car, bus, shuttle, electric bike

Eating: Pigeon peas, citrus fruits, tomatoes, garlic, bottled water, rum punch, sea moss

Packing: Bathing suit, towel, snorkeling equipment, cotton clothing

Suggested: Biking, hiking, entertainment venues, swimming

Anguilla is a British Overseas Territory in the Eastern Caribbean. It's one main island and a few offshore islets. The beaches here are long and sandy, like Rendezvous Bay, which is not too far from St. Martin Island. They are full of secluded caves, such as at Little Bay. There are also many protected areas, including Big Spring Cave, former prehistoric petroglyphs, and a wildlife conservation site.

Fifteen thousand people live on the main island, and it's not as congested as many other islands. There are fewer places to stay and only a few hotels on the small island. Anguilla's Capital is The Valley. What makes Anguilla's beaches the best in the world? White, powdery sand stretching for miles, pristine waters, and the laid-back, welcoming attitude of the Anguillan people. Swim and sunbathe all day—and all year round—at romantic public beaches like the aptly-named Rendezvous Bay, then dance to calypso music at Anguilla's annual summer festival.

Anguilla is a safe island, probably the safest in the region. There are many other islands where you would not go out at night nor feel free to explore anywhere, even during the day.

Travelbest: While Anguilla may require more cash and a few more steps to visit, I think it's worth it. Some of the most beautiful beaches on the island rival the scenery in Bora Bora, Tahiti, which says a lot. Plus, the people are friendly, and the food is fantastic. It's also extremely safe to rent a car and explore.

Do spend time on pristine beaches and relax.

Don't forget they drive on the left side of the road.

4
CHALLENGING SOLO TRAVEL STEP 4

This chapter covers travels for more than a month, multiple places, language barriers, England, Australia, New Zealand, Spain, Mexico, Costa Rica, France, and Germany.

Step 4 is challenging for the solo traveler. Step 4 means you have completed several independent trips already, and this challenging step means you may be entering a country with some language barriers. Step 4 is the second to last step of the solo travel steps. It will be the final step for most travelers because it's a big step to getting here. Step 4 is for the experienced traveler. As a step 4 traveler, you must have mastered the art of going places with your personal itinerary, even if it's just for part of the trip. You've learned how to make travel mistakes and recover from them. By this step, you've learned from your lessons. Step 4 will still take extra courage and added financial planning, but you can plan a quicker trip for just a few days ahead instead of weeks or months, leading us to freedom in Step 5.

Germany is on this list because English speakers can travel to some parts of Germany without speaking German. In the larger cities, you can find English language guidance. Most of the people who live there speak English as a second language. All these trips will require a passport, and some will need a visa. If you have less than six months left on your passport, you should apply for a new one before taking the trip.

Step 4 is for the solo traveler who wants to explore new countries and may not need to be proficient in the country's language. Like Germany, English-speaking travelers may discover several European countries which don't require you to speak their language to travel solo. In Step 4, you will take a trip to Ireland, where you'll be driving on the left side of the road. Most people speak English and have similar customs and heritage to other European and American countries. Gaelic is the traditional language, but most people speak English.

Finding your way around takes minimal prior logistic planning. Step 4 has these other characteristics:

- ☐ Maps are easy to read. You can identify geographic and industrial landmarks. You will figure out where to enjoy the sights and the people. Or you may choose an alternative adventure away from the crowds.

- ☐ You can ride city buses and trains easily because they are primarily marked in your native language.

- ☐ You can purchase the things you need to get along, such as food and shelter.

- ☐ You can connect your language translator app when you need it.

England

Sleeping: hotel, Airbnb, hostel

Transportation: the tube, buses, Taxi, rideshare

Eating: steak and kidney pie, shepherd's pie, bangers and mash, fish and chips, Sunday roast, clotted cream, black pudding hash, Dover sole, mince pie, bone marrow, Cornish biscuits, Billingsgate Fish Market (Trafalgar Way), afternoon tea

Packing: Raincoat, boots, scarf, layers

Suggested: Shakespeare in the Park, Windsor Castle, Buckingham Fountain, British Museum, Tower of London, Thames River, futball (soccer)

When you visit London, England, get the 2-day bus pass which allows you to jump on and off if you can and if the weather is pleasant. You may choose fewer destinations and indoor adventures if it's raining, and it rains a lot. The double-decker buses help you navigate and quickly understand the city. If you are new to London, you will be impressed. You can see the sights in London: Shakespeare in the Park, Windsor Castle, Buckingham Fountain, The British Museum, changing of the guard, and the Tower of London. Since London is the capital of England and the United Kingdom, visit The Houses of Parliament and the nearby Big Ben clock tower and Westminster Abbey. These institutions impact the country's history so see if you can make the time to visit. These are all easy to find for the solo traveler. The main waterway, the Thames River, will help orient your geography. There is an observation deck called the London Eye (as in you can 'see' it), a wheel that provides panoramic views of the South

Bank cultural complex and the whole city of London itself.

Things to do in London will vary depending on your interests. You can travel by bicycle, car, taxi, mini double-decker bus, or on the tube, which is what Londoners call their subway system. There's much to explore for your first trip abroad easily. Shakespeare in the Park is always a good idea if the weather cooperates. Visit Oxford University, which is not too far from London, for a side trip by train. Music and music fests may be your delight, or perhaps art galleries. Sports: Futbol, cricket (Like in Ted Lasso). London has a culture you will like if you enjoy good music and theater.

Travelbest: My favorite museum in London is the British Museum, with all the mummies, plus the Rosetta Stone and Gutenberg Bible. I felt at home in London on my first trip and acclimated to the culture as it was not so different from what I expected. The USA broke away from the British rule in the Revolutionary War, so there is much history between our countries and governments. My ancestors are from Ireland and perhaps Scotland. My grandfather was not fond of the British and let others know about this. The city has many artistic sides to it, including the scenes of music from the Beatles, David Bowie, and Elton John. The British rock band The Who was one of my favorite bands from England.

Do see a play or a musical.

Don't get caught in the rain without an umbrella.

Australia

Sleeping: Airbnb, hotel, hostel
Transportation: car, buses, plane, train

Eating: abalone, carpetbag steak, kangaroo, macadamia nuts, Sydney rock oysters, tiger prawn, vegemite, wattleseed, emu, barramundi, banana, kiwi, apples, papaya

Packing: cold weather: warm jackets. hot weather: light blouses

Suggested: Sydney Opera House, Cruise the harbor, Cairns, Ayers Rock, Uluru

Sydney

Sydney's most famous iconic image is the Opera House— you should not miss it. I toured it and saw a ballet rehearsal for the Hunchback of Notre Dame. It's a very imposing building, which looks like sails in three parts. It's very large inside, and the sound in the concert hall is fantastic. Take a guided boat tour of the Sydney Harbor to learn about the city's history. Even on a cloudy day, you can still see a lot here. The Captain Cook Coffee Cruise was a delight. The bridges were just as you have seen them from afar, only much more authentic from a closer view. This was a neighborhood-like city with welcoming places, including Kings Cross, which reminded me of Greenwich Village in New York City. People-watching is a must-do. You can do this over tea or beer. You can learn about the locals and culture from the pubs. There were enough souvenirs for me and those at home. By daylight and by night, you'll fall in love with Sydney. It's expensive, so be aware of the high costs in such a lovely town.

Gold Coast

North of Sydney is the Gold Coast, a destination worth seeing for the beaches and surf culture. Compared with Sydney, it's a casual, laid-back way of life. Brisbane's Lone Pine Sanctuary has koalas you can hold in your hands. The rainforest surrounds the area with vineyards, and the town is friendly. Kookaburras are here, along with saltwater crocodiles who live in the ocean and rivers. Kookaburras are native to Australia and New Guinea. They are stout birds with medium-length tails and broad, thick beaks—darker at the top and lighter at the bottom. They say kookaburras signify a time of signals and omens, a time to transform your pain into happiness and focus on your family.

Few Aussies have traveled all over their country. There are fewer airlines in this country compared to the size of the geography, like the USA. Chinese food is outstanding. Cairns is where you find the Great Barrier Reef, so take time to visit some of the islands off the coast. Scuba diving here is very popular, so if you like being underwater, you will like this. Anyone who can swim can snorkel on the reef.

Travelbest: I spent about a dozen days in Australia in 1982. My father had been stationed there in the Navy, so it had always been a dream of mine to see this country. I found many souvenirs at the Paddington Market. I started and ended my trip in Sydney and got to see a great deal of the nations. I couldn't find a place to sleep in Brisbane, so I slept in a high school gym, but I had reasonable accommodations for the rest of the trip.

Ayers Rock, (Uluru)

Ayers Rock is in the outback in the Northern Territory, and the closest city to it, Alice Springs, is six hours away. It's a long drive from Alice Springs to Ayers Rock through the bush country. Depending on the amount of rain, this can look barren or colorful. You can fly directly to Uluru, about 3 hours and 15 minutes from Sydney. Even if you can't climb the rock anymore, you can still become inspired and awed by the colorful palate of nature throughout the day.

Although you can no longer climb the rock because the land is sacred to the native people, there's a lot to see here. Walk through the gorge with new friends from Australia and around the world. The site has no air pollution, clouds, or competing light, so in the evening sky, the stars are brilliant. The culture here is all about Uluru, the native people from the area. Their folk music is worth a listen. You'll need to see the sunrise, even in the cold desert morning weather conditions. Aboriginal artifacts like boomerangs and weapons can be seen in the region. From light to dark and every color in between, you will find much peace at this spot. It's a desert-like town and a global village of travelers. Twelve miles southwest of Ayers Rock are more dome formations which are also bright at sunset, called The Olgas.

Travelbest: When I visited the Aussie Outback, you could still climb Ayers Rock. I watched Ayers Rock change color from the Sunset Strip, with about 250 others viewing. It's one of the most photographed rocks in the world. These rock formations are sacred to the traditional local owners of the land. I watched a slide show about the area, then went out for a moonlight drive to see the rock under the stars. Although you can no longer do this because the land is sacred to the native people, it was one of my most exciting and fun adventures. I had such a clear view of the horizon from the top of the rock after the climb. From the bottom of the rock, I followed a white dotted line to get to the top; I sang songs such as "Waltzing Matilda" and kookaburra songs walking along the path. This made my heart light and the journey easier. Back in Alice Springs, I found a desert-like town and a global village of travelers. It was a bit like a mini-Las Vegas with a casino in the desert, only on a much smaller scale.

Do get to know some of the Aussies on your visit. They are friendly.

Don't complain about the dust in the outback. It's part of the experience.

New Zealand

Sleeping: hotels, Airbnb, hostels

Transportation: plane, train, bus, car, motorhome

Eating: pavlova (meringue), Afghan biscuits, green-lipped mussels, Hokey Pokey Ice Cream, kiwi, mouse traps

Packing: can be four seasons in one day

Suggested: Queenstown, Black sand beaches, Rotorua, Wellington boardwalk, Franz Josef Glacier, Milford Sound

North Island

New Zealand (NZ) culture includes delightful legends of the Māori, how New Zealand was discovered, hot thermal pools, geysers, and crafts. Some of the regions sound British, and others seem native Māori. The two letters "WH" sound like F in the Māori language. There are surfing beaches around the area, including one with black sand beaches on one side and white sand on the other, whichever you prefer. Lots of people are renting motor homes for their holidays in New Zealand. Native New Zealanders are on a 6-week holiday in the Christmas summer months, the opposite weather from the Northern Hemisphere. The weather could change quickly on you, so packing for all four seasons in a day would be helpful. Rotorua is home to many mountain biking fans. What I remember most about the town is the strong sulfur smell, like rotten eggs, from geothermal activity and hot springs that come from deep below the earth's surface. You will get used to the smell after a day.

If you go to NZ North Island, you'll hear about the Waikato River, the longest river in NZ, which is 264 miles long. You may find a lovely rural area in Ohakune. In Wellington, on the north island, it's nice to walk on the boardwalk and stroll the restaurants and waterfront bars. Tourist places include the Lord of the Rings filming sights and the Peter Jackson-owned Weta Studios in Wellington.

Travelbest: It rained every day I was there, and I drank a lot of tea. Auckland is a large and bustling city, and I saw it from the 8th-floor dayroom at the downtown hospital, which was a good vantage point. I was not there for a medical reason. I saw the Harbor Bridge, principal streets, and topography from my location. You can quickly drive around Queen Street, past theaters, shops, the university, and the harbor. I ate mouse traps, which were bread with meatloaf and melted cheese. I got to sleep in a local Kiwi home with a 73-year-old grandmother who had detailed stories of World War II and the US military soldiers with whom she had been friends since the war. She radiated kindness, warmth, and love. If you're lucky like I was, you'll be talking to a shearer of lambs and learning about sheep and farming in New Zealand. My friend, Jenny

Latto, is an artist who lives in Waiuku, Auckland City, an hour's drive to Auckland Central or downtown.

South Island

Check the South Island map of New Zealand and how green it is. One city you may have heard of is Christchurch. It made the global headlines when there was a big earthquake and a massacre. Christchurch has warmer weather than Auckland since it's not surrounded by water. If you have limited time in New Zealand, visit Milford Sound, not far from Queenstown on the western side of the South Island. One of my worldly traveled friends told me he thinks it's the best part of the earth in natural beauty. In many ways, this area has similar sights to Norway. The boat trip through the fjords was somewhat magical. The waterfalls are stunning.

In Franz Josef Glacier, you can see the ice formations firsthand and up close. You start as a passenger in a plane on land, and minutes later, you find yourself walking on the top of the glacier.

The Franz Josef Glacier is one of the steepest glaciers in New Zealand, descending from its origins high in the Southern Alps, deep into the lush native rainforest of Westland's National Park. It also moves faster than your average glacier. This creates incredible features in the glacier, such as ice caves, tunnels, and crevasses, which are constantly changing and evolving, so no two days are ever the same. If you have time, ride a chairlift above the town in Queenstown and take in the view.

Travelbest: When I visited New Zealand, I flew Air New Zealand Airlines and loved the service from start to finish. I flew all over the country, and it was easy to get around and lovely to see all the sheep. Once you can travel there, be sure to give yourself time to get to know the people and the beauty there.

Do take a boat cruise in the Milford Sound.
Don't forget there are more sheep than people in New Zealand.

Germany

Sleeping: Hotel, Airbnb, hostel, cabin
Transportation: car, train, bike, bus
Eating: beer, sausage, currywurst, wiener schnitzel, sauerbraten, rouladen, bratwurst, sauerkraut, kartoffelpuffer, spätzle, wine
Packing: warm weather clothes for winter, light clothes in summer
Suggested: Hofbräuhaus, Black Forest, Dachau, Brandenburg Gate, Checkpoint Charlie, cuckoo-clocks, churches

Berlin

Berlin is the city of freedom and the capital of Germany. It dates to the 13th century and is memorable in 20th-century histories for the turbulence. You can visit the Holocaust memorial and the remains of the Berlin Wall. The 18th-century Brandenburg Gate symbolizes the reunification of the divided city. It's also known for the arts and modern landmarks like the gold-colored, swoop-roofed Berliner Philharmonic, which was opened in 1963.

The Brandenburg Gate is Berlin's most popular attraction. It was built in 1791. Back then, it was just one of many old city gates in a medium-sized city. The Pariser Platz was laid at the foot of the gate and now is home to many buildings, like the Hotel Adlon and the Academy of the Arts. The Reichstag is the Federal Government building with a glass dome and a bird's eye view of the city in the Government District. East Berlin was built up fast once the wall came down. Then President Reagan told Russia's President, Mr. Gorbachev, that the wall would need to be brought down. East Berlin was built up fast once the wall came down. Checkpoint Charlie was the most famous crossing point from West to East Germany. Things are different now. You can visit a museum at Checkpoint Charlie. The town is modern and secure. The population of East Berlin is about 4 million people, and no wall exists. It's easy to get around the city, and many people speak English.

Travelbest: I remember going to Checkpoint Charlie to see East Berlin when it was behind the infamous wall. I was scared and nervous crossing into East Berlin in 1986. With sweaty palms and an accelerated heart rate, but excited when I entered this border crossing with one girlfriend traveler. We were solo travelers looking for a history lesson. Back then, there was a stark difference between the two countries, separated by only a gate, as East Germany was very poor, and there were shortages of food and other necessities.

Do see the Brandenburg Gate.

Don't miss the modern-looking East Berlin region.

Ireland

Sleeping: hotel, hostel, Airbnb

Transportation: car, train, bus, rideshare

Eating: oatmeal porridge, seed cake, corned beef & cabbage, soda bread, Irish Whiskey cheesecake, beer, potatoes, black and white pudding

Packing: raincoat, umbrella, warm clothes,

Suggested: Ring of Kerry, Cork, Kinsale, Dublin, Connemara

Ireland is a stopover place for US airlines to Europe, and you can pick up a Ryanair flight to get around neighboring countries. Ireland is similar in size to the US state of Ohio, with half the population of only 5 million people. One in 8 Americans has Irish ancestry, including me at 95% Irish.

If you have three days, start on the east, in Dublin, explore Galway for a day, and sites in between. To get the "Country" experience, fly into Shannon airport on the west side. On my sister Ellen's Dublin visit, she stayed in a suburb and took a commuter bus, which was less stressful and faster than driving a private car. She loved the remote parts of Ireland the best. Aran Islands, Blasket

Islands, and Doolin, just north of the Cliffs of Moher, are a favorite small town. People try to gather nightly in neighborhoods to watch the sunset. Achill Island is stunning and not too far from Westport. She went to Kylemore Abbey more than once. There is a beautiful garden and a great walking path on the property. Many Irish lighthouses include Mizen Head SW and Malin Head NW.

Driving a car in Ireland

Get the best possible insurance. Check your insurance at home before you travel. Get damage insurance. You are likely to get the vehicle damaged. Ask for walkaway insurance. Driving is a two-person sport. Two people will be required for safer left-hand driving. "Left near" and "right far" is how the passenger can coach the driver when making turns. Roundabouts in Ireland are plentiful. Be prepared for the livestock on the road. Driving is difficult and demands your attention to override your instincts to drive on the right side on narrow roads. It is stressful for the passenger as you are sitting where you usually drive in the USA. Be careful crossing streets as you must look right instead of your instinct to look left. Assume you will get lost; leave plenty of time to get lost, even if you have GPS in your car. Some places and roads have more than one name, which can create confusion and increase frustration if you get uptight about getting lost.

Travelbest: When I think of Ireland, I think of the color Kelly Green. I had an airport stop there on my way to southern Spain. One in 8 Americans has Irish ancestry, including me at 95% Irish. Ellen gave me tips on travel in Ireland as she's been there often. She says to determine my priority and work with this goal in mind, as in other travel planning. The number of available days to travel will help you decide what to do with your time. Ellen and her husband spent ten days in each quadrant of Ireland (over four years) and felt like this was a wonderful place. Irish locals would apologize to her for the rain, and she would respond with, "We are on vacation in Ireland!"—rain can't dampen this blessing!"

Do kiss the Blarney Stone in Cork.

Don't believe all the stories you hear.

FAQ: My friend Patti asked me how to book a tour of Ireland and visit her grandfather's old home there if it still exists. She asked me about how to arrange this.

Answer: To find a relative in Ireland, you may start by writing several letters to known relations and asking them to help you find the location. Some parish records could be helpful. Give yourself plenty of preparation. Then you can book your tour after you know your relatives will be around to greet you when you arrive. Enjoy your tour and visit your relatives for a few days after the tour ends. By that time, you'll be feeling warm and cozy about Ireland and able to navigate from one place to another. You can also go to the nearest pub and ask about the relations. If you are lucky, you'll learn about your ancestors and relations from those who knew them. The sooner you do this, the better. In Ireland, they are used to meeting those from the US who are seeking their relations.

France

Sleeping: hotel, hostel, Airbnb, villa, loft

Transportation: car, bus, train, plane, rideshare

Eating: baguette, beef cheeks, truffles, Boeuf Bourguignon (stew), brie, camembert, assiette de charcuterie, macarons, langue de chat, coq au vin, croissants, dijon mustard, foie gras, madeleines, mousse au chocolat, pâte à choux (puff pastry), quiche Lorraine, Roquefort, soufflé

Packing: walking shoes, light clothing in summer, and warm jackets in winter

Suggested: Eiffel Tower, French Riviera, Luchon, Normandy, Omaha Beach, Disneyland, Paris

Paris

France is known for its extraordinary architecture, quaint streets, narrow alleys, and fabulous cafes and restaurants. Beware of the prices because France is somewhat expensive. When you go to Paris, make your reservations for the Eiffel Tower weeks in advance. I could get a reservation at 11:15 pm, several weeks in advance. Book ahead of time. This is a don't miss experience for a solo traveler. If you have an open calendar, visit Paris on June 21 any year and see the city transformed into a musical delight. Every neighborhood has a specific live concert, and all music is free. The tourism board created this experience, and I was fortunate to see it. The French Rivera is a destination for the rich and the famous and has beautiful beaches. You will notice there is a lot of wealth in this area. You will see many yachts and trendy stores. You may venture to nearby Nice, a lovely city along the coast with views that make visitors smile.

Travelbest: I traveled to France for the first time on a budget over an extended weekend. I got a bargain airfare from San Diego to Paris roundtrip, and a friend extended an invitation to stay with her. The trip was to represent the USA. Our USA team competed in the annual Worldwide Competition of Beaujolais Wine Fest event in May in Paris. I represented the USA team and came in second place in this international competition of more than 20 teams. Team USA created a dramatic presentation describing the colorful history and culture of diversity in the United States. The team performed a skit at 41 locations along The Avenue des Champs-Élysées.

Lesson Learned-WIFI troubles in France

I didn't know how to access WIFI for free, except in McDonald's Restaurants in Paris. Whenever I needed Wi-Fi, I went to a McDonald's restaurant. Sometimes it was easy, but other times, it was a challenge to find one. I should have asked for help. I was fearful of looking helpless, even though I was. That was a bad situation, and since then, I have learned a lot more about my settings and Wi-Fi has become more available worldwide.

Normandy

A historic visit to Normandy should be in your future. World War II (WW2) left a significant mark on the country. Visit and see how this part of the world has left a permanent marker of graves which will remind others of how war kills. Located in the northern part of France, you will find Normandy the place to see WW2 beachheads, including Omaha Beach, the site of the D-Day landing. One warning here is don't try to reach this destination on a Sunday, as public transportation is unavailable. Seeing the cemetery at Omaha Beach is breathtaking, and the museum on the grounds is worth it. This part of France belongs to the US.

You'll find other beaches and museums in the region also. The area is tourist-friendly, and most people speak several languages. If time allows, Normandy has the rocky island of Mont Saint Michel, with a soaring Gothic abbey on top. Another suggestion is to find the city of Rouen, with a beautiful cathedral where the Catholic saint Joan of Arc was executed in 1431. You may spend several hours exploring this vibrant region. The vineyards, the alps, and rural towns may be on your bucket list, and if so, be sure to enjoy slow travel there.

Travelbest: My backup plan for solo travel on Sunday to Normandy beaches was to hire a taxi which worked out fine as I recruited another couple of travelers (who had the same issue) who joined my cab, and we split the fare. I stayed in a nearby port city called Caen, the capital of the Calvados department in this region. I explored the Château de Caen in the city, a castle built in the eleventh century by William the Conqueror.

Do visit Omaha Beach.

Don't expect any public transportation on Sundays.

Pyrenees

The region between Spain and France may not be on everyone's travel list, but you may want to consider it for yours to get off the beaten path and away from the big crowds in the main cities of France. Bagneres de Luchon is 50 km southwest of Saint Gaudens and 40 km south of Montrejeau, at the end of a branch line of the Southern Railway at the foot of the central Pyrenees. This is a no-crossing point into Spain, although you can see it from here. The town of Luchon is in a valley at the crossing of the L'One river from the west and the Pique River from the south. The railway station is the (French National Railway Company) SNCF terminal station and connects to Paris.

Travelbest: I took the overnight train from Paris to Luchon, a sleeper car. The train was so relaxing that I almost missed getting off the train and my stop. My Airbnb host met me at the train station and brought me to his establishment. The welcome was sincere and the beginning of friendly hospitality in Luchon, just by the Pyrenees Mountains. The apartment was right off the main center of town, which was quaint and friendly. I went to a French spa in Luchon and got hosed. It was inside a cave which was hundreds of years old, and in one of the rooms, I got blasted with strong water, which was refreshing. I would do it again in a minute.

I went to a nice dinner with my artistic friend and former student from UCSD, Nicole Peyrafitte, ate local food and drank local wines. I also hiked the mountains and visited with some locals at their homes in the mountains, where it felt like I was playing a part in the French version of 'The Sound of Music.'

Do hike the hills around the region.

Don't miss some of the great local foods and wines.

Spain

Sleeping: hotel, Airbnb, motel, hostel, guest house

Transportation: car, bus, taxi, train, bike

Eating: gazpacho, saffron, paella, tapas, tortilla Española, churros, cheeses, capers

Packing: bathing suits, t-shirts and sandals in summer, light jackets in winter

Suggested: Costa del Sol:Nerja: La Alhambra, Granada, Frigliana; Barcelona: Las Ramblas, Sagrada Familia; Madrid: Art Museums

Costa Del Sol

Have you seen the southern coast of Spain? Visit Nerja (pronounced NEAR-HA), about an hour from Malaga, where planes arrive from many European destinations for the warm winter climate. Many Irish and English "winter" here, just like in the USA. Snowbirds from New York and New Jersey often go to Florida for the winter days. The region has a tropical climate, palm trees, and beaches like Burriana Beach. You can enjoy Frigiliana, the Old Town in the area. Churches from the 1600s and narrow streets allowed many tourists to travel, but few cars can drive in town. You will find an old sugar factory converted into a craft store. You can find plenty of souvenirs in this old sugar factory. Another touristy, but worthwhile place to visit is The Caves (Las Cuevas), about 2.5 miles east of Nerja. These were inhabited by man some 20,000 years ago. Some of the wonders here are 32 meters tall from top to bottom. Music and dance were celebrated in these caves back then and even today. Costa del Sol includes nearby Andalucía and Granada, Spain. I visited La Alhambra, a Moorish cultural mecca, a palace from the 13th century. It should take you a full day to explore. I did not need reservations during the low winter seasons, but you should book ahead on a busy holiday, especially in the summer.

You will want to explore the small towns near Nerja, Maro, and Herradura. These are both on the Mediterranean Sea, and very relaxing to enjoy the Mediterranean waters. I went swimming and felt like a mermaid of sorts. It was delightful, even in the off-season of November.

One of the area's traditions is a daily siesta, which you will treasure. Take a nap from 2–4 p.m. and relax your soul. The region near Nerja is called The Balcony of Europe because it juts out into the key, like a balcony over the Mediterranean. See a flamenco performance and visit a Catholic church for mass if you can.

Travelbest: I found the crypts of Queen Isabel and King Ferdinand in downtown Grenada. If you think of Cristopher Columbus, you'll remember them. This busy city only allows local traffic unless you pay extra to drive to the intercity. The city leaders have kept the gridlock from being too congested.

Do see the caves.
Don't forget to take a nap and relax.

Barcelona

Barcelona is the capital of the northern Catalonia region of Spain. The city is world known for art and architecture. You can attend mass for free at the famous Sagrada Familia church. It has limited seating and other buildings by

Antoni Gaudi all over Barcelona. The Museo Picasso and Fundacio Joan (Juan) Miro feature modern art. The history museum, MUHBA, has several Roman archeological sites, and the outdoor markets are special for tasting the culture and current wares of the day. The 1992 Summer Olympics were held near the center of Barcelona, and the athletic grounds are still available to visit. Check any soccer games Barca (FCB team) may play when you visit. You will notice that it's not really "Española" they speak; it's Catalan.

People in Barcelona seem to be more relaxed than in other cities. The outdoor markets have some incredible food treats. Be sure to take a long walk on Las Ramblas, about a mile from the city's center. It's known for pickpockets, so be careful of your valued things like passports and phones. For food, there are paella, Bombas, and plenty of other Catalan delicacies to enjoy. It's a coastal city with a beautiful harbor, convention center, and neighborhoods you will love to walk through. The subway system is easy to navigate, even with a suitcase. Take a trip to the end of the subway line and explore the city. You will find some treasures here and at the markets outdoors.

Travelbest: Barcelona is a better place to visit than the larger city, Madrid, since there is more variety of culture, activities, and architecture. If you must pick just one destination, choose the coastal city of Barcelona. Here, I got involved in traditional dancing outside a church in a public plaza with about 20 total strangers, holding hands in a giant circle, and having so much fun enjoying the music. There was no language barrier here, just harmony and happiness abounded. Since I was alone, I believed I had a destination and a purpose of exploring the ends of the Barcelona inner city, getting out of the subway. If I didn't like the area,   I returned to the subway and visited another neighborhood.

Madrid

Madrid is unique for so many things—like the art museums. It's the capital of Spain and a large, bustling, and busy city. Don't be careless with your personal belongings. Use the city guides and subways to get around. Interact with locals and respect their norms. It's easy to arrive by plane; you can fly on cheap smaller planes between cities, such as Barcelona to Madrid, and back via Ryanair and other airlines servicing these routes. The trains are also good ways to see more of Spain.

Don't eat eggs for breakfast, and don't eat in the Plaza Mayor. Don't be careless with your personal belongings. Use the city guides. Interact with locals and respect their norms. You can fly on cheap smaller planes between cities, such as from Barcelona to Madrid and back. Ryanair and other airlines service these routes. The trains are also good ways to see more of Spain.

Travelbest: I love the historic buildings, sunny blue skies, food markets, and joyful life in neighborhoods. The collections of art from all over Europe spreads throughout the city. I went to all the major art museums for several days and couldn't get enough.

Do eat lunch after 1 pm and dinner before 9 pm.

Don't wear flip-flops unless you are at the pool.

Mexico

Sleeping: hotel, Airbnb, camping, siestas

Transportation: car, bus, train, plane, bike

Eating: Caesar salad, enchiladas, guacamole, huevos rancheros, dulce de leche, empanadas, mole, nopales, tortillas, chili peppers, sopa de tortilla, picadillo, Mexican hot chocolate

Packing: light clothes for summer, winter will require some extra layers of clothing, hiking boots

Suggested: Mexico City: Chapultepec Park, Ballet Folklorico, Basilica of Our Lady of Guadalupe: Puerto Vallarta: Farmer's Markets on Saturday: Ensenada: Valle de Guadalupe, Fresh Fish Market, Estero Beach, La Bufadora

Mexico City

The city has expanded, and there is much to see and do here. More than 9 million people live here, and traffic can be challenging. You must visit

Chapultepec Park and the famous Basilica of Our Lady of Guadalupe, with a capacity of 10,000 people in total. If there's one thing you must do in Mexico City, it's to see the Ballet Folklorico held at the Bellas Artes Theater downtown. You will experience the culture/dance of Mexico. Each scene showcases a part of the culture, history, and geography. For example, in Jalisco, one of the regions of Mexico, there was a cowboy love story, with dancing for all to enjoy. There is no intermission, so enjoy the show and soak it in.

Travelbest: I went to Mexico City for the first time in 1973 and the second time in 2017. They were memorable experiences as both times I was able to experience the Ballet Folklorico. I climbed the Pyramid of the Sun and the Pyramid of the Moon. One of my favorite memories is the song, "La Bamba."

Do visit the Museum of Natural History in Mexico City.
Don't get stuck in traffic.

Baja California and Ensenada

Most people think of Tecate and tequila when they think of Mexico—certainly not wine. But the Valle de Guadalupe, just 90 miles south of San Diego in northern Baja, is a rustic wine destination already being called the 'Napa Valley of Mexico.' The locals say it's better than Napa or Sonoma. The region is one of the fastest-growing wine destinations in the world, with some 150 wineries. Yet, it remains unfussy and relaxed— and every winery offers a distinct experience.

Sip a bright rosé at Vena Cava, a winery constructed from upcycled materials like 1960s fishing boats; sample nebbiolos at Montefiore, a winery owned by an Italian immigrant who brought grapes straight from the motherland; or drink bold tempranillo at Adobe Guadalupe, while feasting on tapas from a food truck. Check out the Guadalupe Valley; it's authentic and not as commercial as Napa. The trip is a day or long weekend from San Diego or Los Angeles. Most of the drive from San Diego to Ensenada is a picture-perfect cruise along the Pacific Coast on a paved toll road. Bumpy dirt roads connect the wineries in the Valley, so ensure your car can handle the terrain. Logistics vary based on whether you are renting a car or driving your vehicle.

- Rental cars: If you rent a car stateside, your rental company might not allow you to drive its vehicle into Mexico. Check with the vendor before renting and prepare to pay an extra fee or put a deposit down on your credit card if the rental is permitted. An alternative is to rent a car in Mexico; know rates posted online often don't include government-mandated insurance.

- Your vehicle: Mexico does not accept US liability insurance or coverage provided by your credit card, so you'll need to buy an additional waiver for your time abroad. Check with your auto insurance provider for a quote on a separate policy for international travel.

The Valle de Guadalupe is close to San Diego, but crossing back into the US often involves long lines and hefty wait times. Aim for travel times outside normal commute times due to the long lines. Many Tijuana residents commute to San Diego for work in the morning and head back to Mexico during the evening rush hour. On the weekends, the rush hours operate in reverse, particularly late-night Saturday, when partiers are heading home, and Sunday afternoon, when weekend visitors are wrapping up their trips.

- Check the US Customs Site: The US Customs and Border Site offers real-time updates on waits for drivers, commercial vehicles, and pedestrian and land ports of entry. Use the site to monitor traffic and head to the border when wait times are minimal.
- Take the Ready Lane: Riders with select identification—including passport cards, Global Entry cards, and Sentri passes—may use the 'Ready Lanes,' slightly faster than the general lanes. The system detects RFID chips in the cards; standard US passports do not comply.
- If you expect to travel across the border frequently, consider applying for a Sentri card, the land-border version of Global Entry. Candidates who pass an advanced screening and pay a fee may use an express entry lane for five years; all passengers in one vehicle must have a Sentri.

With highly educated people and more doctors per capita than any city in the world, Ensenada is known for medical tourism. The harbor and waterfront area are famous, and once a casino, the Riviera de Ensenada is a cultural center now. There are museums and an outdoor fish market which is not to miss.

Ensenada is an 80-mile drive south of San Diego, with all you desire for authentic Mexican food, culture, and nightlife. You will find rest and outdoor recreation, too. The well-known areas of Hussong's Cantina and Papas and Beer tend to have a younger crowd drinking tequila, or you may prefer the vineyards or cellars of Santo Tomas. Gray whales are seen seasonally off the coast as they migrate the western shores to and from Alaska each winter. La Bufadora, or the blowhole, is a massive marine geyser fed by a sea cave & reaches heights of over 100 ft. above sea level. You can listen to the waves going through the blowhole, and it's worth the trip here. Santo Tomas Winery is on the main street east of the Ensenada harbor but within walking distance. You can see what it was like in the early days when altar boys used to serve wine to priests in the church. You can walk downstairs to see the wine cellars here. The restaurant next door is delightful, so make a reservation if you like, in advance.

Travelbest: I hired a minivan and driver to bring a few friends and me to Valle de Guadalupe from San Diego for the day. I've been to Tijuana (TJ) dozens of times, and each time, I seem to get lost driving my car back through town to the border. My favorite Ensenada area hotel is Estero Beach Resort, where you can swim up to the bar and order a soft drink or whatever you prefer. I've been here for surfing, kayaking, mountain biking, and wine tasting. I like to visit The

Door of Faith Orphanage and nearby school for migrant children and serve others when time permits. It's north of Ensenada by about 20 minutes.

Do explore some of the beauty of the coastline in Mexico.
Don't forget to buy Mexican car insurance.

Tijuana

The city is about 15 miles from the San Diego, California border, but a world apart. Passports are required and medical tourism is popular. It's a big city, and it's easy to get lost with so many people and cars. The attractions include Jai alai games, dog or horse races, and a lot of eating and shopping. If you're a shopper, you can visit Plaza Rio or Plaza Mexico. You will enjoy looking at the items in food sections, dreaming of the flavors and smells of the food. The Omnitheatre, in the Tijuana Cultural Center, has a film on a 180-degree screen, so the viewer is right in the middle of the scene, soaring across Mexico, the pyramids, beaches, and cities of today. Forty miles south of Tijuana you will find the city of Rosarito. The Rosarito Beach Hotel is just south of the city, 20 minutes away. Puerto Nuevo is south of Rosarito, famous for lobster served with refried beans, sauce, and tortillas. Ridesharing like Lyft and Uber has made it easier to explore northern Baja, Mexico without a car, even if you're coming from San Diego or Los Angeles. Expect prices to increase for rides involving border crossings, and double-check that your data plan will work in Mexico if you rely on ridesharing.

Puerto Vallarta

One of the favorite destinations for a solo woman traveler is to venture into Mexico, to a city welcoming tourists, like Puerto Vallarta. Puerto Vallarta is a resort town in Jalisco state on Mexico's Pacific coast. It is known for its beaches, water sports, and nightlife scene. Its cobblestone center is home to the ornate Nuestra Señora de Guadalupe church, boutique shops, and a range of restaurants and bars. El Malecón is a beachside promenade with contemporary sculptures, bars, lounges, and nightclubs.

Consider Saturday markets for shopping and some excursions you may want to take. You can also stay at your hotel or cabana and rest. The Saturday Marketing Co-op Pulpito #127 between Amapas and Olas Altas Streets in Puerto Vallarta has fresh loaves of bread, organic veggies, chili, flowers, and arts and crafts. It's open from 9 a.m. to 1 p.m. year-round. It's in the Romantic Zone, also known as the gay district. There's an old Town Farmers Market, and the Esplanade is in the heart of Old Town.

The best time to visit Puerto Vallarta is between April and June when the weather is pleasant and the room rates are affordable. During these months, rain is scarce, and there are fewer tourists compared to the winter high season. If you're interested in whale watching, visit from December to March. Puerto Vallarta is one of Mexico's most affordable coastal towns, with plenty of pristine beaches, street markets, and an Old Town with a Spanish colonial atmosphere. This is generally the most affordable area for accommodations in Puerto Vallarta, and, as a bonus, you're just minutes away from the main beach.

The Church of Our Lady of Guadalupe is locally known as La Iglesia de Nuestra Señora de Guadalupe. It's open daily, with English services on Saturdays and Sundays. It was built in the 1930s on original foundations from a chapel built in 1901. They honor the Virgin Mary, the patron saint of Mexico. She is considered a religious symbol of female empowerment.

Do you want to experience some small group cooking classes in Puerto Vallarta? Chef Mavi (or another chef) will take your group of 2-6 to the various local markets to buy the ingredients (fish market, vegetable market, tortilla market) and bring you to her home for the cooking class.

Travelbest: I enjoyed the Farmer's Market on Saturday. I also like walking along the beach, where hundreds of hotels cater to the area's tourists.

Do spend time relaxing on the beach.

Don't miss the local flavors of the markets and explore a cooking class.

Lesson Learned-Shopping duty- free

When traveling to several countries, I always spent time shopping at duty-free stores for items like jewelry, cosmetics, and other gifts. When I later realized I was paying a premium, I stopped shopping there, except for smaller items. The prices were relatively high in the long run. Watch out for the sign that says "duty-free" because buyers need to be aware, and I was not.

Costa Rica

Sleeping: hotel, hostel, guest house, resort

Transportation: bus, train, plane, bike, taxi

Eating: bananas, pineapples, meat, cheese, pizza

Packing: rain gear, bathing suit, walking shoes, warm weather light clothing for tropical weather

Suggested: zip lining, Poas Volcano, turtles, banana farms, coffee plantations, pineapple farms

If you plan to visit Costa Rica, consider the beach on the west coast, seeing the native animals and plants, and participating in activities like zip lining. You will likely land at the main airport in San Jose, the capital city, and then take a shuttle to your hotel or destination. You may rent a vehicle or take public transportation from the city to a resort. You will feel the humidity immediately, so give yourself time to adjust to tropical weather conditions if you arrive from far away. Drink lots of bottled or purified water to stay hydrated. Have lunch at the Hard Rock Cafe. Visit the Poas Volcano (inactive) as well as some active volcanoes. Hike through a national park, go to La Paz for lunch, and play with butterflies on your fingers and toucans (birds) on your hands and shoulders. Look for frogs, snakes, and jaguars in the wild. Discover at least four kinds of monkeys, cayman (like an alligator), crocodiles, herons, and turtles. Find a zipline and have a forest adventure.

Visitors should explore Tortuga or Turtle Park. The Caribbean East Coast of Costa Rica is a haven for turtles. Turtles here live up to 150 years and have unique migration habits.

You may find an active volcano, a Dole pineapple farm, and a banana plantation. The ocean water here was brown and not for swimming. For refreshment, consider drinking coconut water straight from the shell. Things to bring home as souvenirs from Costa Rica include coffee, chocolate, handmade clothes, wooden items, and jewelry. One of the best times to visit is in January, when the temperature is low in the USA but high in Costa Rica. My friends have gone there for years during the first part of January. This may also be good for you, especially if you live in a city with a colder climate.

Travelbest: I took the Zipline Sarapiqui River Adventure. It was physically challenging. Each zip had something different. Unhook, then hook, then jump, then hook. Never put your hands in front, only behind. I came in backward on some zips. I hit my helmet with the brake. It was something I will never forget from this trip. I'm glad I did it, including the safety training, in advance. In some ways, Costa Rica felt like home to me. It was familiar in an unfamiliar way. I had lunch at the Hard Rock Café; I felt safe there. I walked to a shopping center over a bridge in San Jose and explored the local culture. In a few minutes, I was at a restaurant cheering for Costa Rica during their World Cup soccer championship match.

Do explore the volcanos.

Don't forget to hydrate and say "Pura Vida," which means 'Pure Life.'

Tahiti

Sleeping: hotel, resort, vacation rental

Transportation: Le Truck, taxi, car, boat, ferry, plane

Eating: poisson cru (raw fish salad), Tahitian vanilla, seafood, coconut

Packing: sarong, bathing suits, snorkeling gear, tropical climate clothing

Suggested: black sand beaches, Moorea, Bora Bora, open-air markets in Papeete, snorkeling

Tahiti is famous for its black-sand beaches and for inventing surfing. The sand gets its dark hue from lava, and the color contrast is spectacular at sunset. Riding the open-air buses all over town and drinking from coconuts are good cultural experiences in French Polynesia. Tahiti is a safe place for tourists. However, watch for pickpockets in the capital city, Papeete, and moray eels in the coral reefs during your scuba dives. Most visitors quickly discover Tahiti is warm and welcoming to foreigners. Papeete is the capital city of French Polynesia, an overseas collectivity of the French Republic in the Pacific Ocean, and a group of islands in the South Pacific. Besides the port, the large Marché de Papeete (market) sells local produce, fish, and handicrafts.

Travelbest: I was in Papeete nearly every day of my trip. The Robert Wan Pearl

Museum focuses on the local pearl industry and sells jewelry.

It's hard not to love islands like Morea and Bora Bora. The coral reef serves as a backdrop to the island's lagoon, which earned Bora Bora the nickname "Pearl of the Pacific." I spent one day snorkeling, talking to people from all over the globe, and learning about the culture of Moorea. I slept under the stars and then got drenched when it rained.

Do enjoy your snorkeling.
Don't forget sunscreen or wear a protective layer as the rays are intense in the water.

Lesson Learned-Double check airline ticket

Missing my flight in Tahiti: I missed my flight to Sydney, Australia by 12 hours. With a paper ticket in hand, the travel agent had written 1 p.m., but the flight really left at 1 a.m. I missed the boat, so I took a small plane to get to the main airport, but I missed the flight to Australia, too! The lesson is to double-check airline tickets for the correct day and time.

Fiji

Sleeping: Airbnb, hotel, resort, hostel

Transportation: boat, bus, car

Eating: eggplant curry, ramen noodles, rice, breadfruit, fish, pork curry, taro, cassava, papaya, breadfruit

Packing: sarong, sandals, raingear, bathing suits

Suggested: Island hopping, Sabeto Hot Springs and Mud Pool, Natadola Beach, Fiji Culture Village, kava ceremony, rafting

You will most likely land in Nadi, although the capital is Suva. Head towards one of the 333 islands as quickly as possible. You don't need to make a reservation for most places, but you can if it makes you feel more comfortable. There are two major islands, although there is probably a spot on a small island just waiting for you to relax. You may spend time on Treasure Island and remember saying "Bula" countless times in Fiji. Bula has the same meaning as 'Aloha' in Hawaii or 'Hello.' Get used to it and enjoy the experience. You can learn how to windsurf, snorkel, scuba dive, and hike all over the country.

Travelbest: One of the things I found interesting about Fiji was its Indian influence. Many Indians went there during the British colonial times, so Indian culture became very influential. I remember buying lots of beautiful Indian jewelry and eating delicious Indian food there. You should also definitely visit the beautiful beaches because this is one of the big reasons for going to Fiji.

Do enjoy the island lifestyle.
Don't try to visit every island.

5 FREEDOM TRAVEL STEP 5

This chapter involves the uncharted or unknown, visiting places with foreign languages you don't speak fluently. Africa, Asia, and South America are continents where you can start. Countries such as Kenya, China, South Korea, Japan, Seychelles, and Chile are highlighted in this chapter. Some of these regions will require you to have a visa or travel permit to visit, depending on which country you are from. This is the peak Step, and the most challenging travel destinations are here. Many readers will not make this kind of trip because it really is a big step, and it's always a challenge to learn how much you don't know about a region. I believe this content will interest you even if you never travel to a Step 5 country.

These Step 5 Freedom Travel solo trips are not recommended for most US citizens to visit without first experiencing and enjoying Step 4 travel. Some regions of Asia or Africa may be impossible or unwise to visit, such as countries like North Korea. Step 5 Freedom Travel is about getting out and having unique experiences in nature and cities, in countries with names you may not even know how to spell, and seeing people who are very different from you. If you are heading on a Step 5 journey, I want you to be prepared for anything, including losing your passport, luggage, and cash. You want copies of everything necessary in a safe place and a backup (physical or digital)ready whenever needed.

However, you may combine Step 5 with another step in a hybrid Step 4/5 trip. If you are heading to a country on this list or uncharted to you, prepare all your documents in advance, including your birth certificate, passport, and any required vaccinations. You may need a permit to visit the region, so ask. In Tibet, only tour groups are allowed, and all tourism is subject to frequent closures. For travel to Mongolia, like many other countries, you will need a visa and a passport with more than six months before its expiration date.

I've not been to places that take four days to get to from the US, but they exist on our planet. My friend is a scuba diver who goes to remote locations on small islands in the Indian Ocean. This takes time and energy to plan to make a trip successful. She sometimes travels for up to four days to arrive at her destination. If you're traveling to an especially remote location, consider adding stops to travel around the layover cities.

Africa

Seychelles

Sleeping: hotel, Airbnb
Transportation: rideshare, car, Mini Moke, bicycle, oxen-driven taxi, boat
Eating: Papaya, pineapple, beer,
Packing: Bathing suit, hiking boots, sunscreen, light clothing in summer
Suggested: oxen ride, Mombasa, Scuba diving, nude beaches, tortoises
Seychelles is in the Indian Ocean, off the coast of East Africa, near Madagascar. The best times to visit Seychelles are April, May, October, and November. These months represent the transition times between the hot and humid

northwest trade winds (November through March) and the cooler southeast trade winds from April through October. Seychelles is one thousand miles away from the coast of Kenya, has more than 100 small islands, and is north of Madagascar. The primary language is French Creole, followed by English. You'll find a few things in Seychelles: lush vegetation, Coco de Mer or sea coconuts, tortoises, scuba diving, and nude beaches. Mini mokes (tiny rental car-like jeeps) are like beach buggies you rent to get around on the big island, and oxen are used instead of cars on the smaller islands. The small islands can be reached by boat, which is easy to arrange. The island of La Digue is known for its beaches on the west coast, like Anse Source d'Argent, dotted with granite boulders. To the south, you'd find the isolated Anse Bonnet Carré Beach, with calm, shallow water. Like Anse Cocos beach, it's accessible only on foot. La Digue's diverse wildlife can be seen in the Veuve Nature Reserve.

Travelbest: One of my favorite memories of a week spent here is riding a taxi pulled by an ox. There were no cars on several islands. I recommend visiting the island of La Digue. Some of my best scuba diving was here.

Do rent a mini moke.

Don't expect much traffic.

Kenya

Sleeping: Airbnb, hotel, motel, hostel

Transportation: Car, bike, bus, train

Eating: baobab fruit, Zanzibar duck, coffee, ginger, sesame seeds, beer, ostrich meatballs, crocodile, camel hump, lamb, sausage, ox heart

Packing: bathing suit, long flowy dress, loose clothes

Suggested: Nairobi National Park, Mombasa, Masai Mara, Carnivore restaurant

Nairobi

If escaping the everyday grind is your goal, Nairobi, Kenya, is the place to go. To experience a significant difference in lifestyle, take a flight to Nairobi, the capital of Kenya, and explore the former British colony. Your trip may differ, but here are some things you may encounter. Your first Kenya destination will be a bustling Nairobi airport. Once settled, you can explore Nairobi National Park, located only 10km from the downtown Nairobi area, which I did on my first day in Kenya. You may stay in hostels and hotels here.

The Masai Mara game reserve located in Narok County has the best variety of wildlife, maybe in the world. It's packed in a relatively small area, and travel is best in the fall when game spotting is at its peak. You can take a sunrise balloon ride and end with a champagne breakfast in the reserve.

Animals in the Wild

On safari, you may find yourself in a deluxe tent with a wire fence around it and an employee with a baseball bat who keeps monkeys away. Elephants are known to brush up against the fence, so the job is necessary for visitors' safety and peace of mind.

You can gallop alongside zebras and wildebeest and observe lions in the wild. The Big Five animals to see are lions, elephants, buffalo, leopards, and rhinoceros. Consider participating in a volunteer program such as African Impact, a lion rehabilitation program on game farms.

On this trip, you will experience the rural and coastal low country as well as the plateaus of Nairobi. Louis Leakey's legacy is a good history lesson to understand archaeology in Kenya. You should wear loose clothes that cover your arms and legs. You should not wear shorts. Cotton or linen clothing is recommended. Follow wildlife and customs/immigration rules. Never take pictures of someone without their permission, especially here. Some believe that photography of the person takes part of their soul. Either way, it is an invasion of privacy. Don't carry valuables; preferably, get someone you trust to guide you through the city if possible. You can bargain at the markets for jewelry and other handcrafted items. Most of the time, the prices listed are negotiable.

Corruption can be found here often, so be careful. The police and military have poor reputations for sexual harassment and assault. Theft comes with power here. Others have been jailed for not respecting the currency here, so be warned. The country has good qualities worth the visit, but be careful and stay safe from danger.

Travelbest: My first stop was Nairobi, where I arrived without a hotel reservation or local contacts. I was grateful to have met some new friends on my journey, who helped me learn the dos and don'ts of the region. They offered me a place to store my belongings while on safari. My trip to Masai Mara included an airplane built in the 1940s circling a cement area until the zebra cleared the runway.

I was served hot breakfast with tea in my safari tent. It was the fanciest tent I could have imagined, including a private flush toilet. For two days, I rode in a jeep with two couples on safari and saw all the major animals in the region. I was able to capture the Big Five on video, including lions, elephants, buffalo, leopards, and rhinoceros. I spent a month exploring Africa, primarily by myself. It was one of my most defining trips because I was outside my comfort zone and did not speak to anyone I had known before from my home country. Being so isolated was a personal lesson in survival. I was warned not to remove any money from Kenya. I forgot, and the airport guard discovered my cash and kept it for himself. I had no recourse to report it.

Do become acclimated to the lower oxygen levels at this high elevation.
Don't take anyone's picture without permission. Don't remove currency from the country.

Lessons Learned-Getting a lousy travel roommate

When you travel, sometimes you may get stuck with a bad roommate. I was in Kenya and nervous about getting malaria. During the middle of the night, the other resident guest opened the room window and let the mosquitos in, causing me to get lots of bites. I switched rooms the next day. I had taken malaria prevention tabs ahead of time, so I was ok, but it was a lesson learned.

Mombasa

Mombasa is a tropical coastal city in Kenya, along the Indian Ocean. It's the country's oldest and second-largest city, after Nairobi. You can get here by road, train, or air. The Standard Gauge Railway has made the train much easier to travel from Nairobi. The population is about 1.2 million, and it's a beach city. The most significant for a visitor is malaria, a disease transmitted by mosquitoes. Before your visit, take the malaria medication prescribed by a physician.

The locals in Kenya live a rural existence. The Masai culture is full of dance, and a simple way of life. Tourism is a big business here. Mombasa has a blend of people from India, Arabia, and Africa in this city's melting pot. It is the best coastal town to explore in Kenya. You can visit the Fort Jesus Museum and see the famous elephant tusks and monuments to the illegal ivory trade. You can also walk through Old Town and spend time at the beach. Check the state department travel advisory before you travel to Kenya.

Travelbest: I took the sleeper train from the city of Nairobi, which starts at a mile-high elevation and ends at sea in Mombasa. The train to Mombasa from Nairobi was one adventure I want to encourage you to explore. For me, it was a 15-hour overnight trip. Today's high-speed train has cut the time to less than 5 hours. I noticed a boat with the nonprofit global organization C.A.R.E. stamped on it. When I asked, I was told these donated goods would be re-sold back to the people in Kenya for profit to the politicians. The ship came from Somalia, the country just north of Kenya. I spent a month here and found this destination to be one of my most incredible travel experiences.

Do explore the beaches.

Don't forget that mosquitoes transmit malaria.

Advice- Jet Lag Tips

Get on the schedule of where you will be a couple of days early. Need a way to limit your jetlag? How about an app? Here are some suggested apps.

Timeshifter. Timeshifter is an app that helps resynchronize your circadian clock with your new time zone through a unique sleep, light, and caffeine schedule.

Also try Jet Lag Rooster, Sleep Cycle, and Uplift

Asia

China

Sleeping: hotel, motel, guest house, inn

Transportation: Bicycle, train, bus, car, plane,

Eating: Asian pear, dim sum, Hoisin Sauce, Birds nest soup, chow mein, Kai-Pai-Ku (barbequed spareribs), candied apple fritters, Peking duck, water chestnuts, tree ear mushrooms, Sichuan cold jellyfish salad, rice in South, noodles in the North

Packing: warm jackets, boots and gloves in the winter, light linens in summer,

Suggested: Shanghai: Peace Hotel, the Bund, Century Park

Beijing: Great Wall of China, Beijing Zoo, the Forbidden City

Hong Kong (East Asia): Gondola Ride, boat trip to Kowloon, The Peak Morning Trail

East Asia

Here is how to plan your visit to East Asia solo. First, you need to get a visa, so you will need at least seven months on your passport to send it to the embassy. You will choose "vacation" travel on the visa application, where you can indicate the name and address of a hotel when you have a reservation, as the application will require this specific information. The best time to go is during the off-season, September through December, because the crowds are smaller, not during Chinese New Year (two weeks in January/February). Avoid traveling during the hot and humid months of July and August. If you can stay for a month or more, good for you. China offers a 10-year visa for US passport holders, allowing you to enter the country as many times as you want for an entire decade. If you apply for this kind of visa, it might be more expensive, but well worth it if you want to return more than once.

Select a mix of famous and not-so-popular places that are not on the list of most prominent cities. See the smaller towns, if you can, located ten or more miles away from the main rail stations. Riding the train in China is a ground-level view of the geography and culture. The high-speed rails whisk you along the countryside, and you will see China which few others experience. You can travel on the train from Guangzhou to Shanghai in about 8 hours, and the cost is very reasonable. The train stations are immense. Pay extra attention to your train number, the platform you're on, and the signage in the station. Colorful signs can give you directions, but they're not usually in English. Several airline carriers from many cities fly direct to China. Find your flights from your favorite online travel agency.

Take the gondola ride to the top of the tallest hill. You will meet people who speak English in Hong Kong. Take the ferry around the Hong Kong islands. The city will be bustling. In Hong Kong, dim sum is traditionally eaten for breakfast or lunch, so you'll get the freshest pickings earlier in the day. Dim sum is a type of food, not the name of a specific dish. You can ask the host or hostess for popular recommendations, but note restaurants might try to sell you more than you can eat. If you are solo, you can do whatever you think will make your visit to China the most memorable. Consider a hobby or a particular area of interest.

Travelbest: Here is what I did to prepare for a solo trip to East Asia. When I graduated from my global doctoral program and worked at a TV station, I dreamed about research and traveling. I considered visiting Asia and made this a reality once I booked my hotel reservation at the Great Wall Sheraton, Beijing. I got a visa from my congressman in Washington, DC. I purchased an airline ticket to Hong Kong on Cathay Pacific Airlines. I bought one-way tickets from Hong Kong to Beijing, Beijing to Shanghai, Shanghai to Hong Kong, Hong Kong to Taipei, Taipei to Hong Kong, and finally, Hong Kong to San Diego. I arrived in Hong Kong and found a taxi to a neighborhood where I walked around and found a cheap hotel for two nights. There was no hot water, but I didn't care. The following day, I woke up and started exploring the city.

I wrote letters to the leading advertising companies and TV stations ahead of time, asking if I could visit them. One particular TV station was the friendliest and most inviting of all. I made some friends and learned a lot about how they sell commercial airtime in Hong Kong, since my role in business resembled this career at the time. I focused my energy on understanding how the Superbowl in 1988 was being presented in China since it was going to be "live" on Hong Kong TV from my current hometown, San Diego. The day before I flew home, I watched the TV show live from the Hong Kong Stock Exchange building at a fancy buffet breakfast. It was in English, with exciting Chinese commercials. I still have the recording of this telecast on VHS video; I converted it from PAL format. I've shown it in my college classes on advertising dozens of times since then. I met with several ad agencies and PR firms in Hong Kong. I went to the horse races, which I found were off-track betting. I rode in a taxi, the subway, the bus, the boats, and the gondola.

My first trip to East Asia was in the 1980s, following my mom's inspiration, as she had already been to China on her own—smuggling Bibles. Highlights of my solo visit were seeing Beijing before the Tiananmen Square Revolution, getting a private tour behind the scenes at the Hall of the People and walking along the Great Wall of China, seeing the Pandas in the Beijing Zoo, and the delights of the city life in Hong Kong and Shanghai. My next visit was 30 years later, as a business consultant to a Chinese firm, and a visiting professor, teaching Marketing to Graduate business MBA students at Sun Yat-Sen University in Guangzhou.

Do enjoy tea at the Peninsula Hotel.
Don't forget you are a visitor and respect the history of East Asia.

Beijing

The Chinese built the world's largest airport in the southern part of Beijing in 2019. It's grown since 1988 from the one terminal that could handle 12 planes. The panda exhibit in the zoo was empty of visitors, with no one in line to see them. In San Diego, you'd wait hours to see the pandas at the world-famous San Diego Zoo. What a contrast! If I were returning to Beijing today, I would spend my time in Tiananmen Square. The main tourist areas begin at the Great Wall, seeing the tombs, the Forbidden City, and the Summer Palace. There is so much to see and do in Beijing today.

Travelbest: I flew from Hong Kong to Beijing. I was the only American whom I noticed at the airport. Arriving in the city alone, I took a taxi to my hotel, the Great Wall Sheraton. This was an impressive experience because it was grand and impressive coming from the drabness of the city proper. In Beijing, everything looked drab green. No one wore colorful clothing. I located the Chinese tour offices where a friend of a friend worked.

Seeing Beijing

The tour guide came out to meet me. He offered to give me a full day's tour with one other person. We spent a full day at the Great Wall, seeing the tombs, the Forbidden City, the Summer Palace, and the behind-the-scenes, and then having lunch and dinner together. I could see the remains of the body of China's leader, Deng Xiaoping, who had died the year before. His body was on display in Tiananmen Square, enclosed in glass. This was six months before the historical protests of the government in 1989. My tour director friend had special privileges to visit behind the scenes, so I could see what few people did—the riches and the extravagant gifts others had given China over the centuries. It was so impressive to see history come to life here. Having the introduction from a friend made a big difference in my trip. It was cold in

January. I stood out because of my height. There was a hepatitis breakout during my visit, and no vaccine was available. I was told not to shake hands or eat out. However, I did not have a choice. I had to eat out. There were no places to buy snacks. There were markets where you could buy food in bulk, but not a corner 7-11. Not then, anyway. My second hotel in Beijing overlooked the square. I could walk there and spend time videotaping the sights and hearing the sounds.

Do visit Tiananmen Square.

Don't expect to have flush toilets everywhere you visit. Do purchase packets of tissues to bring to the bathroom; they usually won't provide toilet paper in public areas!

Lesson learned-Getting a haircut in Hong Kong:

It was too short. I looked like a man. When I tried to get a bathing suit in a hotel, they gave me a men's bathing suit, not a woman's. This was not acceptable, but I had to live with it until the hair grew back in. If you get a haircut in a country where you don't speak the language, provide a photo of your desired look.

Shanghai

Today in Shanghai, several dozen buildings are over 100 stories high. The streets have cars instead of bicycles. There is commerce everywhere you look, and at least one convenience store on every corner. Riding the train in China is a treat if it is an upper-class carriage. The lower-class ones are horrendous. There is rarely any English in the train stations, so figuring out where to go and how to buy a train ticket is challenging. The younger Chinese are more likely to speak English, so you may approach them for train information or to request to write down the place you want to go in Chinese characters. The cities like Shanghai in China have older pockets of their ancient parts within them. When you visit, you can look for the hidden old city, just a few blocks from the new skyscrapers.

Travelbest: This was January 1988, and Pudong, on the East side of Shanghai was still small in acres—a farming community was just five minutes from the city. The tallest buildings were only 10 to 20 stories tall. When I went back in 2017, the skyline was different. In 1988, my USA college professor gave me the names of two American women, Robin and Marty. I went to meet them at the Peace Hotel in Shanghai. They were running an import/export company as CEO and CFO. They knew logistics and shipping, so they were successful with clients such as REI and Patagonia. They were friendly and invited me to join their large Shanghai ex-pats group.

I remember walking into a store shopping for souvenirs and being approached by a local man who spoke English. He had relatives in Seattle and was hoping to move there someday. Even though visitors were not allowed in Chinese homes at the time, he invited me to visit his home in Shanghai, but I had to be very quiet for him to sneak me in. There were neighborhood watch people who would report him if he was caught. I did visit his house and met his wife and children for several hours. This was scary and a bold, brave move. It gave me a lot of insight to learn firsthand about the culture, lifestyle, and interests of the Chinese people.

When I went out to eat in China, I got the menu but could not read it. I would point to something others would eat and order, not knowing what it was.

Lesson Learned- Getting lost in Shanghai on a bike.

I went out for a bike ride in Shanghai with millions of bikers in 1988. I was lost in the dark on the way back to town; it was rush hour. Finally, I found someone to whom I could flash the peace sign, who showed me the way to my destination, the Peace Hotel. I visited the same Peace Hotel 30 years later, and it's still a landmark.

Travelbest: In 2019, I flew from SD to LA to Guangzhou by myself again. This city was very progressive. I taught Mobile Marketing to university students, including many of the case studies from my textbook. They taught me a lot about apps, including how they used WeChat for all their purchases and banking. They never carried any cash; all they needed was their phone. I ate all my meals with them on campus and went to the teacher's lounge to play ping pong at night. Due to the firewall in mainland China, many social media platforms used globally are not found in China, so they have their own versions for most apps. To cross this firewall, before you arrive, you must get a Virtual Private Network (VPN) to access everything on the internet and stay connected.

Do take a ride in an elevator to see the skyline of Shanghai.

Don't get a haircut if you don't speak the language.

Korea

Incheon Airport, Korea

Sleeping: pod, couch

Transportation: bus, escalator

Eating: Bulgogi, Korean pancakes, kimbap, spicy rice cakes, burgers, kimchi tofu soup (sundubu), beer and fried chicken, black bean noodles, pork cutlets, Korean fried chicken

Packing: warm clothing for winter travel, light clothes for summer

Suggested Museum of Korean Culture, K-pop, beauty stores, coffee houses, or Krispy Kreme, musical concerts

Incheon International Airport (IIA) is the largest airport in South Korea and one of the largest and busiest in the world, ranked the world's cleanest airport and best international transit airport by Skytrax. It has a golf course, spa, private sleeping rooms, an ice-skating rink, a casino, indoor gardens, a video game center, and a Museum of Korean Culture. The airport holds a record of being ranked the Best Airport Worldwide for 11 consecutive years by the Airports Council International (ACI). To be ready for the future growth of Korea, the airport opened in March 2001, serving many areas, including Tokyo, Osaka, Beijing, Shanghai, and Taipei. It was created by building an artificial land between two islands, initially separated by a shallow sea. It has 111 boarding gates.

This airport is layover heaven. They have it all. Free showers at Incheon make such a difference on a long journey. The airport supplies towels, soap, shampoo, a hairdryer, and hot water! There were sleeping areas, like little pods, and plenty of free touchscreen computers. The ambient music was delightful; there was a baby grand piano and professional musicians. In the Cultural Center, you can design a keychain with the mother of pearl and other jewels. There was a center to try a new technology from Korean companies that you could demo. One was an immersive flying experience.

The duty-free shopping mall has been rated the world's best for several years. Duty-free shopping is better than most airports. There was a Prayer Room and a Korean Airlines Premiere lounge, with a public lounge for $50. However, only Korean credit cards were accepted here.

If you want to go to Seoul, you'll take a bus or a train from Incheon Airport to the capital city. Estimated travel time should take an hour or less; public transportation on buses, subways, and trains in South Korea makes it an attractive tourist destination.

Travelbest: For shopping, I sampled many items and saw a lot of unique products for sale. I bought Korean skin care products and Korean food. I bought recommended honey butter-flavored chips. My Korean dinner was kimchi, steak, chicken tenders, veggies, mango/lemon drinks, and tangerines. I was in the airport for a five-hour layover on the way to Taiwan and another seven hours on the return. The shower before my return flight made me feel much better because I had become run down with all my traveling and was worn out. After the shower, I felt refreshed.

Do take a shower and sleep in a pod.

Don't miss your flight because you're having a good time here.

Thailand

Sleeping: Airbnb, hotel, guest house, hard mattresses, sleeping in public acceptable

Transportation: train, subway, bus, taxi, rideshare, rickshaw, boat

Eating: Kaeng (curries), coconut, mee krab (crisp noodles), sangkhaya (coconut custard), Sriracha sauce, Thai mussels, tom kha gai (coconut kitchen soup), Indian food, pad thai, fresh and dried mango

Packing loose clothing for the tropics, rain gear, umbrella

Suggested: massages as often as possible, Chiang Mai, Phuket, Krabi, flower markets

Thailand is a fast-growing country, covering a lot of areas and a Step 5. The most popular tourist regions include Bangkok in the central area, Chiang Mai in the north, and Phuket and Krabi in the south. The weather is tropical and hot, nearly 90 degrees F in January. The people in Thailand are known for great hospitality and tourism. You will find it easy to speak in English and be understood frequently by people on the streets of big, crowded cities like Bangkok, the capital. Bangkok is a sprawling city. At first, it's hard to understand how vast this tropical city is. Boat cruises on the rivers are one way to see many parts of the city and feel a cool breeze as the boat moves over the water. Visitors should not speak ill of the Thai Royal Family. So, it's probably best to not mention the family.

Getting around on public transportation is best with refillable Bangkok Transit System (BTS) cards, called Rabbit Cards, as auto traffic is jammed up most of the time. Both ancient temples and modern shopping malls stand side by side as a contrast. Another contrast is that Buddhist monks, those in massage, and the red-light district share the same city streets. Massages in Bangkok for an hour cost about $6 to $10 each, depending on your service request. Bangkok is a sprawling city. It's hard to get a grip on how big it was. Boat cruises on the rivers are an excellent way to see many parts of the city at a reasonable pace.

For a treat, have a formal tea at the Mandarin Oriental. The Mandarin was right on the river and delightfully peaceful. You will enjoy the satay or the yellow curry. You should order Pad Thai, of course, and fresh mangos or desserts when you eat out. Shopping for souvenirs is cheaper here than in most Step 5 countries, but you should be careful to check the quality of what you buy. Don't miss the Flower Markets and wholesale warehouses near the fruit market. You can visit this on your own any time of the day. Spend as much time as you can, soaking in all the smells and colors, enjoying a pleasant summer in the middle of winter.

Travelbest: At the Temple of Dawn, I was asked to cover my legs past my knees, so I bought a second pair of pants to wear over my first. I ate dinner at an Indian Restaurant; Bukhora's was good Indian Food. I saw a local pop-up bar in a VW bus. The entire minibus was transformed into an outdoor commercial bar at night and converted back into a parked VW bus during the day. I took the wrong BTS twice throughout my stay and went to all but two of 35 BTS stops in Bangkok. There were rooftop decks for lap swimming at two places where I stayed. One rooftop pool required a fingerprint password to enable access, so the property owner had their personal fingerprints embedded in a fake plastic finger. This experience with a fingerprint reminded me of a James Bond movie with espionage all around the hotel. The swims were refreshing in this humid paradise.

Do take a boat ride.

Don't miss out on a daily massage.

Lesson Learned- Wearing the wrong length pants in Thailand.

Cover your legs. When you visit Thailand, you must cover your legs entirely when visiting certain places, especially religious temples. I had on what to me were pants, as they covered my knee and then some. However, the temple people told me I had to wear pants, so I went to the outdoor market and bought a pair which went over my regular pants, so I wore two layers. These new pants cost about one dollar, and they make for pajamas now and an excellent memory. Wear long pants when visiting a temple.

Taiwan

Taipei

Sleeping: Airbnb, hotel

Transportation: train, bus, taxi

Eating: Niu Rou Tang (beef noodle soup), sheng jian bao (fried dumplings),), oolong tea, papaya milk, starfish, tropical fruits, bubble milk tea, Japanese hot pot, Chou Dou Fu (stinky tofu), salty-sweet basil, garlic and scallion pancakes, BianDang (traditional bento lunchbox)

Packing: raingear, umbrella, tropical weather clothing spring to fall, coats in

winter

Suggested: Taoyuan City, National Palace, night markets, Jiufen, New Taipei City, Taipei 101, DanShui Station

If you are thinking about visiting Taiwan, here are some suggestions for what to do. Taiwan is also called the Republic of China. Once you arrive, plan to visit green spaces around the city. For one capital city, Taipei is close to nature and offers an incredible mix of cultures. You can visit the Taiwan universities near the Taipei Zoo, including National Chengchi University and National Taiwan University. Many people in Taiwan will want to speak to you to practice their English. Walking around the campuses at the universities may inspire learning some Mandarin words.

History of China in Taiwan

The National Palace is worth seeing in Taipei. An olive pit carved into a boat with doors was one small, impressive item. It's as tiny as your pinky fingernail. It also had people, a poem, and detailed writing on the pit. Something as small as a pit can become a work of art. The best artifacts from mainland China are in Taiwan at the National Palace, and most of these items arrived in 1948 with those who left the mainland country for a better life. There is much to see on this island nation. Another historical monument is Chiang Kai Shek Memorial Hall, which is worth a visit. There are art exhibits located beneath this Memorial Hall, which change every few months. If you're lucky, you might be able to attend a musical performance at the National Concert Hall just across the lawn.

The local Taiwanese usually walk or bike around Daan Park in Taipei to get outdoors. Worth a good long visit is Yangmingshan National Park. It is one of nine national parks in Taiwan, known for cherry blossoms, hot springs, sulfur deposits, fumaroles, and hiking trails. You may find some resort-like bathhouses and sulfur springs in the areas nearby, especially in Beitou.

A train ride away from Taipei is Jiufen, where narrow streets, food stalls, and sweeping views of the mountains and sea attract many tourists. You may find a lovely teahouse to spend the day. The Japanese first built this city as an old gold-mining town. Notice the Japanese architecture when you visit. Another memorable area is the Taroko National Park on the east coast of Taiwan. The gorge is a treasure to hike and explore on foot, by bus, or by car. A public bus system can take you from Hualien (the nearest train station) all the way through Taroko Park on a circular loop.

Most international airplane traffic to Taiwan arrives in Taoyuan City, so you may want to stay here instead of in Taipei for a slower pace. Another slice of life is on the west side, Zhuwei Fish Harbor, near Taoyuan City, just a drive or train from Taipei. Right from the boats, you will see some unusual kinds of fish and shellfish for sale. It's easy to walk around the fish market, and you will be glad you saw the variety and freshness of the seafood.

Hot pot dinners are a Taiwan treat. For this eating style, select uncooked food from a buffet, bring it to your designated hot pot at your table, and cook it yourself. For an after-dinner treat, try the dessert at Ice Monster, a flavored ice cream made from fresh fruit and homemade ingredients for milky shaved ice.

Flavors range from fresh mango to boba milk tea to sesame and almond milk. You will find tasty and unusual food items at night markets in RaoHe, Dongan, Shilin, NingXiaMarket, and Taipei.

The East Coast of Taiwan is famous for its scenery; you have an unobstructed view of the Pacific Ocean for lovely stretches on trains and along the highway. You won't want to fall asleep on the train, as it's truly breathtaking to watch. Book a train in the evening to watch the sunset from the train cabin or stop at one of these coastal cities for a night near the beach. Cities like YiLan, Hualien, and TaiDong (Taitung) are known to welcome foreign visitors.

Travelbest: I went to Yehliu Geopark near Keelung City on my first visit to Taiwan in 1988. At the seashore, the rocks were unique, washed by years of ocean exposure. It reminded me of a tree forest, except the statues were coming out of the rocks, not land, and were rocks themselves. There's an aquarium and several nicer restaurants in the area to visit if you want to extend your stay.

My first time in the Night Market, I saw people drinking snake and turtle blood, which I thought was incredible. I did eat frog legs here for the first time; they tasted like chicken. My daughter, Cate, has lived in Taipei for more than four years. My son, Brian, my daughter, Tina, and I have spent time in Taiwan. Brian traveled south to Kaohsiung City, where he met his friend/roommate's extended family. He said train travel there was easy, even without speaking the language. This city rarely has American visitors, so he was treated in many respectful ways. When I return, I plan to visit the Lambai (XiaoLiuQiu) and Green islands in southern Taiwan.

Do use the subway to get around the cities quickly.

Don't expect the cab drivers to speak English or see English menus outside

Taipei.

Japan

Sleeping: Airbnb, hotel, futon on tatami mats or ashitsuki (legs attached) ryokan, traditional inns

Transportation: trains, most well-known is the shinkansen (bullet train). In order of slow to fast speeds: local (kakueki-teisha or futsu-densha), rapid (kaisoku), express (kyuko), limited express (tokkyu), super express (shinkansen)

Eating: Hotels have a buffet breakfast, which includes a lot of different types of Japanese foods, sushi, yakitori, tempura, sashimi, bento, edamame, fugu, hiyayakko (chilled tofu), loquat, boba, wasabi, kyuri (cucumber), matsutake mushrooms, miso soup

Packing: comfortable shoes for long walks. Sweaters for cool nights. Jackets in winter

Suggested: Tokyo: Todai University, Skytree Tower; Sapporo: Sapporo Beer Factory, downtown clock tower and park; Kyoto: Temples; Hiroshima: site of the atomic bombing

Japanese culture is unique because they were isolated on their islands for so long; the art, the music, and the business customs are worth exploring. They have unique ways of cooking, dressing, and worshiping.

Tokyo

Tokyo Skytree (the highest point in Japan) was built in 2010. The University of Tokyo, abbreviated as Todai or UTokyo, is a public research university located in Bunkyo, Tokyo, Japan. Established in 1877 as the first imperial university, it is one of Japan's most prestigious universities.

The toilets are high-tech. They have heated seats with bidets, and even mimic the noise of flushing water, so others won't hear you in the restroom. They measure a lot of things, such as water temperature and flushing pressure. Some cost up to $6,000 and are advanced technology.

Hiroshima

Hiroshima is a modern city on Japan's Honshu Island, largely destroyed by an atomic bomb during World War II. Today, Hiroshima Peace Memorial Park commemorates the 1945 event. The ruins of Genbaku Dome are in the park. Genbaku Dome was one of the few buildings left standing near ground zero. Other prominent sites include Shukkei-en, a formal Japanese garden, and Hiroshima Castle—a fortress surrounded by a moat and a park.

Sapporo

Sapporo is the capital of the mountainous Japanese island Hokkaidō and is famous for its beer, skiing, and annual Sapporo Snow Festival featuring enormous ice sculptures. Every winter, it snows here, and every February, they hold a Winter event full of sculptures, skating, and natural snow beauty. Milk products are high quality in Hokkaidō and make good gifts to bring back home. Hot sake, or atsukan as the Japanese call it, helps you stay warm during a cold day. With about 2 million people, you can get around here quickly by bus, car, taxi, and subway. I could walk to many places as I stayed near the city's center. As a solo traveler, I found it easy to get around the city's subway system on my own, even without speaking the language.

The Sapporo Beer Museum is in the Sapporo Garden Park in Higashi-ka, Sapporo, Hokkaido, Japan. The Sapporo Beer Museum traces the city's brewing history and has tastings and a beer garden that you will find easily. Be sure to take the tour because it's more than just about beer, but about the culture of the people and history. The Sapporo Beer Museum is in the Sapporo Garden Park in Higashi-ku, Sapporo, Hokkaidō, Japan. The museum is the only beer museum in Japan. It was registered as one of the Hokkaidō Heritage sites.

Ski hills and jumps from the 1972 Winter Olympics are scattered within the city limits, and Niseko, a renowned ski resort, is nearby. You can visit the Olympic Village and see the ski jumps and the virtual ski and toboggan runs for visitors to have a hands-on experience, in any season of the year.

Odori Park is a mile-long urban park that slices through the modern skyscrapers, cutting the city into north and south. It's an oasis in the city with 92 types of trees, including lilacs and elm stands, located right in the middle of a business district. Spend time here if you can and soak up nature. At the eastern edge of the park, you will find a clock tower, and you can ascend the building and see the view of the city from here. Sunset would be an exceptional experience; you can see the mountains overlooking the city in the distance.

Susukino is a bustling city neighborhood with entertainment at a fast pace, like New York City, only smaller. As a traveler, you will find plenty of green spaces with that balance between nature and nurture.

Visit the Fushimi Inari Shrine and follow the large red Torii gates through the "tunnel" that symbolizes the passage from earthly life into the sacred afterlife. You can leave a prayer or an ema, written on a card and hang it with the others in the shrine. The region's history is preserved in outdoor parks, museums, and universities. Asahiyama Memorial Park is atop the city, with a good view or visit Nakajima Park, with sweet-smelling fragrances.

Big breakfasts are on tap daily at the leading hotels, so you can sample a little bit of all the food types, especially miso ramen and hot sake. Noodle lovers are thrilled here. All-you-can-eat breakfasts, a traditional Japanese breakfast, is likely different from any other breakfast you'll ever experience. Typically, a traditional Japanese breakfast consists of steamed rice, miso soup, a protein such as grilled fish, and various side dishes. Familiar side dishes may include tsukemono (Japanese pickles), nori (dried seasoned seaweed), natto (fermented soybeans), kobachi (small side dishes which usually consist of vegetables), and a green salad. Although a Japanese breakfast comprises what Westerners might view as a complete meal appropriate for lunch or dinner, it is not intended to be heavy or too filling. Portion sizes for breakfast are adjusted to meet one's appetite, and dishes tend to be lighter; for example, they tend not to be greasy, deep-fried, or rich.

Travelbest: I visited the island of Hokkaidō in the northern part of Japan a few years ago and fell for the region as it is an outdoor city in many ways. Hokkaidō Museum and Hokkaidō University, with beautiful vegetable gardens and brick buildings of higher learning were worth exploring while I was on my own and had a chance to experience this area.

Do enjoy a large breakfast.

Don't miss the beer factory.

Kyoto

Kyoto, Japan, has become known as the cultural and historical center of the country. You can experience temples, gardens, geisha, festivals, shrines, shops, and restaurants. You can take a Raku Bus with many typical tourist destinations for tourists in Kyoto. They accept one-day city bus passes and Kansai thru passes, and it will be easy for Step 5 travelers to navigate on their own without a guide. One of your first stops in Kyoto will be Nijo Park and Nijo Castle. It's been a UNESCO World Heritage site since 1994 and includes six buildings and a very scenic spot. It was built in 1603 as the official Kyoto residence of the first Tokugawa Shogun, Ieyasu. It has examples of the early Edo period and Momoyama culture, with the era's paintings, carvings, and designs. It's called Nijojo.

Next, you will want to visit The Kinkakuji Temple, the Golden Pavilion in the Northwestern part of the city. It was formerly called Rokuonji and housed the relics of Buddha. The garden and pavilion represent the Pure Land of Buddha in this world. Like Nijo castle, it became a World Cultural Heritage site in 1994. Gold foil on lacquer covers the upper two levels of Kinkaku, and a shining phoenix stands on top of the shingled roof. The teahouse is worth seeing, too. The third stop may be the Heian Jingu Shrine, on the east side, which is more centrally located. See Igashi Hongani Temple; in the southern part of the city. The Kamo River divides the city between east and West and is a beautiful walking spot. In summer, restaurants open balconies looking out to the river. Pathways run along the river, and some stepping stones cross the river.

Travelbest: See the Kyoto National Museum; I stayed at the Hyatt Regency Kyoto, nearby. I also visited Tokajomyooin Temple, Kiyomizudera Temple, Jishu Shrine and other memorable places of worship.

Do visit the temples and castles.
Don't expect the Japanese traditions to be the same as yours.

Lesson Learned- Clueless in a nude bath in Japan

I was alone in a hotel bath in Japan. I am unfamiliar with this and needed to learn what the protocol was. The water was warm, and I love to swim, so I went in without the proper bathing routine. The appropriate way is to enter naked, rinse your body first, and then enter the water. I felt very uneasy because there was no one to follow or ask a question about how to go about this, but I figured it out the second time I went back and saw how it was done. Ask ahead of time if you're going to a bath. Don't be like me and try to wing it.

South America

Chile

Sleeping: hotel, hostel, Airbnb,

Transportation: train, bus, subway

Eating: Empanadas, chili peppers, matambre (stuffed flank steak) asado, meals with locals, restaurants

Packing: be prepared for any weather conditions, snow in mountains, hot in deserts

Suggested: skiing at Portillo, wineries, casinos, resorts

South America is the opposite season from North America for weather conditions. Chile is a very long and narrow country, covering many miles north and south. Many believe Chile is a destination for excellent travel all year long. The people are simple and generous, like those from small towns in the US. They don't speak much English, but you can communicate with some basic language skills, and hand signals help. Try to learn some basic Spanish if you can, especially to count to ten, which will help you count money, an essential skill for a traveler in Step 5. The residents in remote areas of Chile meet few people outside South America. You may be the first person they meet from North America or another continent.

There are many resorts, and skiing is typical in the Andes Mountains in Chile. Los Farallones and El Colorado, two Chilean resorts, were combined into one,

so you could ski from one resort downhill to the other. Chile is a beautiful destination, even if you don't speak Spanish. The mountains are wonderful to experience but driving down steep icy, snowy roads with hairpin turns can get very scary in a snowstorm, so be prepared for dangerous conditions.

Travelbest: I took a day-long solo public bus trip around Valparaiso, near

Santiago, Chile. I met a youth of about ten years old on the bus who invited me to his mother's home for lunch. I was the first-ever North American in their home. I also skied at Valle Nevado. Coming down the mountain was one of the scariest moments of my life. There were 33 hairpin turns and a single lane without guardrails. You can ski there in July, and I was skiing with the USA ski team at Portillo.

Do explore the region of Santiago, Chile, and the neighboring city of Valparaiso.

Don't forget to learn some Spanish phrases to make your Step 5 trip better.

6 TRAVEL FAQ'S, LESSONS, AND ADVICE

FAQ- What should you bring on an airplane for a 5-hour or more extended flight? Bring your small luggage and place that in the overhead compartment if you can. Put your small bag by your feet to access the things to use on the flight.

FAQ- What should be in your small bag? Your sweater, snacks, chewing gum, water bottle, phone, earbuds, phone charger, toothbrush and floss, and something to read. It would help if you wore warm socks to prevent cold feet. Airlines don't always have blankets and pillows anymore. Noise-canceling headphones may be the best device you invest in for a long flight. And consider eye covers and a pillow for your neck if you want to sleep. Even If you checked your bag, you might want to have a change of underwear and a t-shirt in case your luggage gets misplaced.

Bring your food on the airplane to be sure you get what you want and when you want it. What works well is dried fruit or nuts and a sandwich. Southwest Airlines no longer gives out peanuts due to allergies. Today, as I write this, I was given a choice of Ritz Cheese crackers, Oreos, and corn chips. These are not very healthy options, especially on a five-hour cross-country flight.

Be sure to stay hydrated. You lose water when you fly. It's dry, even if you don't feel it. The longer your flight, the more water intake you need.

Be sure to consider your destination and the temperature there. When you depart from the plane, you may find that the weather is much different. If you are heading to a cold weather climate, have a warm coat with you and if you go to a hot/ humid destination, be prepared to remove layers or change to shorts or a skirt.

FAQ- What are AirTags? The AirTag is a small tracking device developed by Apple, to act as a key finder, which helps people find personal items, such as luggage, keys, or other essential items.

FAQ- Should I join the frequent flier program tied in with my airline? Credit cards have the best programs without expiration dates. Hotels and airlines have expiration dates on their mileage reward programs. The answer depends on the cost and if you will get any value back. There are many choices besides airlines that offer incentives for travel rewards. The rules change frequently, so here are some highlights as of this publication date. Here are a few choices from the major US airlines.

Alaska Airlines is affiliated with Bank of America. Their mileage program offers an annual companion ticket, but you still need to pay $99 plus the taxes and fees. To qualify, you must spend a certain amount of money within the first few months of owning the card. You are working for the card while the companies get to keep and repurpose (i.e., sell) your data and spending information. It may take six months or more to deliver your credentials. Then you can book a ticket with a companion. Do you want to wait six months? You can buy tickets up to 300 days in advance, and the pricing is only sometimes the best available. *Southwest Airlines Rapid Rewards* is affiliated with Chase Banks. Their program offers four different levels of credit cards (Priority, Premiere, Plus, and Business). You earn points with their partner brands, too. The Companion Fare Program comes with an annual fee, and one companion may join you on every trip once you qualify and where seats are available. *United Airlines* has loyalty programs. You pay a primary credit card fee annually. *Delta Airlines* has a good mileage program overall. It would be best if you fly often or forfeit the miles. With all these choices, check the disclaimers for restrictions.

FAQ: If there's a flight delay or cancellation, what can I do about it? When the airline cancels, you could be entitled to either a ticket refund or a replacement flight. These rules are all subject to change. You could claim compensation if the airline informed you of the cancellation less than 14 days before the scheduled departure date. The payment amount varies, depending on the distance of the flight. You are entitled to refreshments and beverages during long waiting periods. If you cancel the flight, you should check with the airline for their current rules, as there could be a cancellation or change fee.

Advice- Raise your hand to switch seats if needed If you are in an aisle seat with an empty seat next to you, and someone asks you to switch seats so a parent and child can sit together, go ahead, and offer. You never know how you can make someone's day by doing small things like this. Offer to help someone who needs support, and you will feel good about that move during and after your flight.

FAQ- You asked about solo travel, without your family. Is that wrong? It's a personal choice, so think about it. Do you have someone to care for your family while you travel? Will they be able to feed, dress and take care of themselves without you? If you can say yes to these questions, you should be able to make the trip. You can make the solo trip you always wanted to take.

Advice- Plan some things and leave a lot of unplanned days on your trip for some spontaneity. You don't need to have a new destination every day. You may want to stay longer, linger, and enjoy the roses. Give yourself time to get to know your destination before you depart.

Advice- Sun Rash can go south fast-Protect your skin from Sun Rash and Heat Rash. Adjust your timetable if you are not used to being in the sun. Go out in the early and late hours of the day and stay indoors mid-day. When you visit places where it's even more than 100 degrees Fahrenheit, sleep, or siesta in the midday for your best health. Heat rash is a dangerous side effect.

Lesson Learned- Oversleeping I overslept when I had an early morning airline flight. It's easy to do because I tend to stay up late, not sleep well, and feel restless the day before a long plane trip. Please don't do what I did. Set several alarms, so you don't oversleep. Be self-reliant about your trip. When you are solo, you don't have a backup person. It's all up to you.

Advice- Unplug from the stress of travel when you can Unplug yourself from the many creature comforts and technology at your fingertips. Spend your time and money wisely and buy something that no one can ever take from you, memories. I don't necessarily think that you should jump out of a plane like George Bush did two times. But you can experience a lot using your senses while in an airport, train, car, and on foot.

Lesson Learned- Losing photos I've lost a lot of digital photos. Please Don't do what I did. Download your images to a thumb drive or external drive, so you can retrieve them easily next time. Please don't wait until it's too late. Make sure you do this regularly, at least twice a year.

Advice- Smartphone settings Ask if you need clarification about Wi-Fi,

Bluetooth, and Cellular options. Know how to set up a Personal Hotspot if you need to access your laptop, too. Keep your master password up to date, and once you have that, you should be able to access all passwords. Consider a VPN (Virtual Private Network) for an extra layer of security.

Advice- Hydration-Bring one or two empty water bottles when you travel. Fill them up at the airport after you clear TSA, get to a new destination, or after heavy exercise. Stay hydrated while you travel, especially on a long drive or flight, as you will deplete your water supply, especially on hot days or in the tropics.

FAQ- I'm recently single, and I want to travel more. How can I get the group rate even when I travel solo?

One way to qualify for the group rate is to offer to share a room. You may be asked to pay a single supplement if you are on a tour. Some tour groups don't charge this fee, but you must shop around.

Advice- Confirm your flight at least a day in advance.

If you confirm your flight, you will have more confidence in your trip. Find out where your flight is using the latest tools, including FlightAware.

FAQ- Do you have any tips to help me find my destination when I travel solo?

The answer is Google Maps, MapQuest, Waze, or other navigation apps on your phone provide real-time navigational aids, but if you can't use them for whatever reason, here are a few tips. The sun rises in the east and sets in the west. When facing west, south is on your left. Another idea: Practice with your Compass App, which comes installed on your mobile phone under "Tools." If you haven't used it lately, open that app and practice with navigation and direction. It will also give you the elevation and the coordinates of latitude and longitude. Spin it around and see the change in the dial.

Advice- Travel inspires Travel gives me pleasure, knowledge, cultural awareness, social outlet, spiritual expression, and more.

FAQ- How can I avoid the back row on the plane?

Book your seat early if you can. Before you book, you can review the airplane itself and determine the best seating. You are not guaranteed the seat, even if you are given that on your reservation. Be sure to arrive at the gate on time, so you don't give up your seat.

Advice- Be kinder Be a little kinder to your service team wherever you travel. They have had some tough times over the past few years, so give them an extra smile, grace, and kindness. It will go a long way because they've never been in this situation before; try using more patience and kindness.

FAQ- Can you recommend a good money belt? I am afraid of being robbed and want to be safer. My sister Ellen keeps her passport, cash, and extra credit card in her RFID-blocking money belt. She hooks it to her backpack at night, so there is no way it can be left behind after she checks out of her lodging. Wear it under clothes. It is comforting to both the body and the spirit, knowing that a pickpocketing incident won't occur. There are several, including the camo pink color ones on your favorite shopping app for under $20. Sizes are adjustable.

Lesson Learned- Check your tickets, especially airline tickets

I should have checked the airline changes to my travel flights added significant unwanted delays. Airlines can change your flights, and they do. They can give you a 23- hour layover, and they did that to me on at least one occasion. And I noticed the delay when I tried to board my plane. The connecting flight was not until the next day, they told me. This was in Toronto, returning from France. I was stuck for another day, and of course, there was nothing that I could do but give it one more day. I was with Tina, my daughter. I got a taxi to a hotel and spent the night there. I was exhausted anyway, so one more night wasn't too bad.

Advice- Try something different this time on your flight reservations. Book two one-way tickets instead of a round-trip ticket. Book one way instead of a round-trip ticket. You may enjoy the travel more and can use different airlines. You can fly into one airport and out of another to provide flexibility and save time in returning to the original airport. One-way tickets may be more costly, but they may be a good option if you have a limited travel duration.

FAQ- Where can I learn about the local arts before visiting? What is the best way to soak in the culture, especially if you don't know where to begin?

Start by reading a lot and a little planning. Which arts most interest you? Is it music? If so, you should consider some live music on your trip. If you like sculpture, find out the best-known or most exciting sculpture and seek that out. Suppose you prefer to dance; research where the live dances are. If you want to see a film, you seek out those opportunities, which may be at a drive-in theatre. Culture is a beautiful way to learn about a region, even if it is close to home.

Lesson Learned- Don't expose your new camera or tech in a crime-ridden neighborhood. A friend exposed her camera to the community unknowingly. She was taking photos with an expensive camera in a bad neighborhood in Brazil but needed to be made aware of the reputation. She was too focused on her project and should have been paying attention to the surroundings. Her camera bag was open, and she was not protected. A nice person walked up to her and said that she should not be exposing this beautiful new camera to the public in this area, known for nearby thieves. She thanked the nice person and left safely.

Advice- Clean your best feature with care and love Wash your face every night with cold water and moisturize with whatever you have. It will make you feel good now and when you awaken.

CONCLUDING REMARKS:

Be sustainable in your thoughts, actions, and meaning.

Start small. Little things make a difference as they add up on your travels.

Slow travel is good travel.

"There is no shame in prioritizing and slowing down vs. overdoing. Most injuries happen when people are rushing." (Ellen McCabe, sister)

Why You Should Go:

Why should you go and keep saying "yes" because you know you should?

ACKNOWLEDGEMENTS

Special thanks to Tina Shubat, Catherine Shubat, Ellen McCabe, Sandra Holloway, Shareen Grogan, Rich Griffin, Martin Banks, and Anastasia Stebner. Book Beta readers: Liz Myers (my high school English teacher), Kathy Tiernan, Raquel Giraldez, Leslie Joseph, Liz Tansill McGrath, Jill Curtiss, Cindy Clark, Nancy Castaldo, Angali Bhardwaj, Alice Daly, Peggy Lee Ranke, Lori Carter, and countless others.

Global editors from 12+ countries:

Shareen Grogan (US), Katrina Pla (Spain), Joy O. (Kenya), Victoria Guerra. (Chile), Johanna Higgs (Australia), Cynthia Nnadi (Nigeria), Jennylin Garcia and Ma Jimlet (Philippines), Maria (Columbia), Abigail Gordon (Jamaica), Anjali B. (India), Muzaffar Faqir (Pakistan) and Rebecca   Crowe   (UK)

RESOURCES

Caruana, Robert; Crane, Andrew & Fitchett, James (2008). Paradoxes of consumer independence: a critical discourse analysis of the independent traveler. *Marketing Theory*. Volume 8(3): 253–272

Caruana, Robert & Crane, A. (2011) Getting Away from It All: Exploring Freedom in Tourism. *Annals of Tourism Research*, Volume 38, Issue 4, Pages 1495-1515, ISSN 0160-7383

deBecker, Gavin (1997) *The Gift of Fear: Survival Skills that Protect us from Violence*. Dell Publishing.

Humes, E. (2016). *Door to door: the magnificent, maddening, mysterious world of transportation* (First edition). Harper, An Imprint of HarperCollins Publishers.

Hyde, Kenneth & Lawson, Rob (2008) T1 - *The Nature of Independent Travel Journal of Travel Research*

Theroux, Paul (2011) The TAO of TRAVEL, HMH

Tinling, Marion (1989) *Women into the Unknown: A Sourcebook on Women Explorers and Travelers,* Greenwood Press, Westport, CONN.

Urry, J. (1990). The `Consumption' of Tourism. *Sociology, 24*(1), 23–35.

ABOUT THE AUTHOR

Dr. Travelbest wrote and self-published ***The World's First Guide to Independent Travel*** (1993) as a world travel guide and sold more than 10,000 copies through book signings at the Air and Space Museum in Balboa Park and Yosemite National Park's Ansel Adams Bookstore. Since this publication, more than 100 million miles have been recorded by people who have read, listened to the podcasts, and followed on social media—people who are going places on planes, trains, autos, bikes, boats, and on foot, and one day in space.

5 Steps to Solo Travel, Part A: A Women's Guide to Travel in Her Prime is for women who need confidence and how-to-travel guidance. ***Part B: A Women's Guide to Destinations in Her Prime*** released in 2022. The pseudonym "Dr. Travelbest." will be continued by daughter and avid global traveler and contributor, Dr. Christina Shubat—and loved by future generations of travelers.

Dr. Mary Beth McCabe has a Doctor of Business Administration (DBA) degree from Alliant International University and founded a marketing and media agency in 1993, serving Fortune 500 companies with cross-cultural marketing and digital strategies. She is a world-renowned business leader in marketing and a professor at ten universities, currently teaching at Point Loma Nazarene University. In addition, she has traveled to all 50 US states and major cities, including rural regions and over 30 countries. She has traveled solo or with a friend to six continents. She is co-author of Mobile Marketing Essentials (Stukent, Inc.), the world's first textbook on Mobile Marketing. She lives in San Diego with her husband, Allen. Their four adult children are traveling while working and advancing their education.

Made in the USA
Columbia, SC
26 February 2024

32031186R00109